When Men Have Miscarriages:

Finding Hope Amidst Silent Pain

Dave Deets

DEDICATION

To Tom, Julie, Megan, and Julia…
most of the world will never know
your self-sacrificing love, selfless devotion,
and gracious, servant hearts.
But to those of us who
are privileged to know you,
we will never be the same.
Thank you for showing us Christ!

CONTENTS

ACKNOWLEDGMENTS

I would like to thank my editor, David Madsen. He has taken my meager writing and made it so much better.

I would also like to thank my good friend, Amy Johnson. Amy has done a masterful job at designing a difficult theme and capturing it with grace. Thank you, Amy, for all your hard work on this project.

I am deeply indebted to Cori Poovey, WHCNP. Cori was graciously willing to lend her medical expertise as an OB/GYN Nurse Practitioner to this project. She was one of the first people to read this project and without her kind, clarifying, and reaffirming comments, this project may not have been completed.

Finally, words fail in expressing my love for Kimberly, Caleb, Andrew, and Rebecca. Thank you for allowing me to tell our story. May the world be blessed because of what we share in this project. I know it is not easy to be in the spotlight.

FOREWORD

This is a short, must-read book for any pastor or small group leader who desires to be better equipped for the work of ministry and to provide support and encouragement to those who walk with us on this journey of life. When discussing the heartbreak of miscarriages and the subject of loss, it is always a challenge to know what to say or how to help. Perhaps you and your spouse or your friends have walked through this deeply challenging and shadowy valley.

When Dave asked me to read his manuscript, I told him in my response that my wife and I had never experienced the grief of miscarriage, and I doubted my ability to have valuable contribution or input. I purposed in my heart to pray about his request, however, and agreed to read the manuscript. I cannot adequately express how much I was affected by what I read—his words impacted my mind and heart in a way I did not expect. While I knew many of my friends had experienced this type of loss, and I knew it must have been hard to work through, I had no idea how difficult such a tragedy event is for a couple to handle together and as individuals I immediately wanted to send the manuscript along to some friends who have experienced this sorrow, and soon I heard how they were greatly encouraged by reading what Dave had written. They agreed that this is a much-needed resource. Several friends told me they wished they had access to a resource like this when they were going through the fire and pain of grief and loss, desperately grappling with emotional and spiritual struggles that were deeply impacting them. There are resources for females dealing with miscarriage, but very few resources are written to men and for men. This book will minister grace to men who are going through this hardship and will also minister grace to their wives.

Dave lays out a brilliant theological and practical foundation for walking with someone through one of the most challenging events that a marriage can (hopefully) endure. His story, while it may seem to be a common one, will most certainly open your eyes to ways you can effectively and lovingly walk alongside a man or woman who is going through such a time. If you are a husband, reading this book may help you be a more understanding shepherd of your wife through a miscarriage. Dave's transparent rendering of his feelings, emotions, and thoughts will illuminate a pathway tearfully trodden by many of our friends or family members. His analysis of the usual, familiar responses as they are viewed from the perspective of pain and confusion will likely alter how you intervene from this point forward. Dave's thoughtful approach to engaging the other children in the family during this time of loss is especially helpful, and I believe reading this book will help to bring much healing within families. A friend or pastor can do much to encourage healing and spiritual growth through a better understanding of the suffering of others, and you will find this book to be a good road map and an excellent resource. My ministry and mindset toward people going through miscarriage will be forever altered by the time invested in reading Dave's work. I am much richer in my ability to influence lives for God's eternal work. I pray this book will be shared widely and that it will minister much grace in the Body of Christ!

Bobby M. Wood, PhD

BACKGROUND

It was a normal Sunday morning. As a pastor, I made it my habit to greet as many people as possible both before and after the service. On this particular Sunday, a lady talked to me about her son and daughter-in-law. She wanted me to pray for them because they were having troubles with their pregnancy, and they had just discovered that the daughter-in-law had just had a miscarriage. This was nothing new as I had had this sort of conversation with numbers of people through the years. This conversation was not much different than the many I had had previously, and my response was similar: a genuine empathy for what they were going through, a caring word or two to comfort the mom who was grieving the loss on behalf of her son and daughter-in-law, and then an assurance that I would, in fact, pray for her and for the couple. That is where normalcy ended.

As was the custom with this particular lady, she and I engaged in a deeper, more theological conversation about the matter. She asked if I knew of any resources I could give—especially to her son, as he was having a particularly difficult time with the miscarriage. I replied in my typical response when asked that question: "No, there really isn't. In fact, there is very little written on the topic for women, let alone for men." And then it happened. She replied with a matter-of-fact response: "Well, someone should write something on this topic." I replied, "Yes, they really should." In and of itself, that conversation was nothing spectacular. What happened next, though, was life changing. As soon as I replied with, "Yes, they really should," it was like a convicting knife to my heart, and I felt the prompting of the Holy Spirit, Who said, "There is absolutely no reason why *you* shouldn't write something on this topic to help guys through the process of miscarriage."

That was seven years ago as of the writing of this book! Seven years it has taken me to get the courage to write something about this topic. Seven years to repeatedly start and then walk away from this project. Seven years to hear more people say, "Well, someone should write something on this topic." Seven years to set aside my own fears of being vulnerable. Seven years of facing my own emotions. Seven years of trying to avoid the reality that I really had never dealt with my own trauma. Seven years to "run" from what I knew God was prompting me to say. Seven years to finally realize that if I am the only one who actually benefited from this project, then it was truly worth it! This book won't take you seven years to read, but I do trust that—as God has helped me—the thoughts, ideas, stories, and Biblical principles contained in this small project will help you or someone you know.

May God help us all, whether young or old, whether we have experienced a single miscarriage or too many to count any more, or whether God has spared us from this unique loss. May God help us learn more of Him, learn more about ourselves, and, ultimately, may He be glorified.

INTRODUCTION

Can we be honest about something? Having a baby is a big deal! Can we also be honest about something else? Guys don't really know how to handle the nine months that lead up to the birth and all the sleepless nights that await the expectant family. We didn't typically spend our lives thinking about children nor the process of being pregnant. We typically didn't go to baby showers, and we typically were completely unaware of any thoughts about pregnancy. So, forgive us, this is a whole new world for all of us as men.

For the most part, guys feel disconnected from the process of pregnancy. Oh, sure, we know in theory about what goes on with morning sickness, and we know about how sometimes the sweet, wonderful woman we married is, well...., not always sweet and wonderful. This is no knock-on women; men would be far worse about the whole pregnancy thing if we had to go through that ourselves. The point is guys don't really know what it is like to be carrying a baby. To be honest, the thought of another human being growing inside of a person kind of weirds us out a little bit, or maybe a lot…okay, it really weirds us out!

As men, we see our wives going through the excitement of finding out they are pregnant and all the joy they experience with that. However, even though we may participate in really elaborate pregnancy announcements or gender reveals, for all practical purposes, we are removed from the moment-by-moment changes that are occurring in a woman's body as the new life begins to not only grow but also affect how the woman feels as well. It isn't that we don't care about the pregnancy or even that we don't care about what the woman is going through; it is just that our bodies aren't going through the same changes as hers are and, so, we become somewhat oblivious to the reality of what is happening.

When a woman is going through the physical and emotional changes of pregnancy, it isn't that guys don't care, it is just that we really have no way of understanding what in the world she is going through. So, when it comes to the unfolding of the pregnancy, we may have had too much pepperoni pizza and Mountain Dew too late at night and experience bloating and discomfort and wild dreams, but that goes away shortly. Guys don't experience much in the way of physical issues unless we decide to gorge ourselves on some wings at B-Dubs.

It is for this reason that virtually every pregnancy book and birth book is geared toward women, and rightly so. Women: a big shout out to you for all that you go through in pregnancy. Speaking for guys everywhere, we are overjoyed that it is you and not us! I know that that is God's design, but, nonetheless, men everywhere are thankful for the fact that you, the woman, is the one who gets to carry the baby. This is how

God designed it and for that we are so thankful.

However, there is an issue within the genre of pregnancy and birth literature that is seldom, if ever, talked about. It is the matter of a miscarriage. Take for instance, this statement from webmd.com:

> A miscarriage is the loss of a baby before the 20th week of pregnancy. The medical term for a miscarriage is spontaneous abortion. But it isn't an abortion in the common meaning of the term. As many as 50% of all pregnancies end in miscarriage—most often before a woman misses a menstrual period or even knows they're pregnant. About 15%-25% of recognized pregnancies will end in a miscarriage. More than 80% of miscarriages happen within the first 3 months of pregnancy.[1]

This means that it is very likely that your wife will lose a pregnancy due to miscarriage and, if she doesn't, you will have a buddy and his wife who goes through that experience. In this seldom-spoken-of topic of miscarriage, any material that is written is geared toward women. Very little, if any at all, is actually written for men. And that is the very reason for this project. My desire is to at least put something out there for men as they process through miscarriage.

It is my goal in this short project to address a subject that very few have written on and address a subject very few want to deal with. The issue is how do we, as men, deal with miscarriage? How do we cope with what we experience and go

---

[1] https://www.webmd.com/baby/guide/pregnancy-miscarriage#1

through in the process? How do we help comfort and encourage our wives when they experience the physical loss of pregnancy? How do we make sure that we cope with the deaths of our children in an appropriate way? Are there emotions and grief that we should be dealing with? Is it wrong for me as a man to feel sad and even heartbroken when it comes to having a miscarriage? Can I just stuff my feelings deep down and act like they don't exist? How about if I just simply ignore the situation all together?

To be clear about the scope of this book, our intent is to address the loss of a pregnancy prior to birth. This book is not intended to address infertility per se or to address the loss of a newborn child at an early age. We concede that the loss experienced in these areas is, in and of itself, devastating and provides unique challenges. Although some of what we address in this project will relate to that, the reason for this narrow scope is that a miscarriage presents an entirely separate aspect of grieving, comparatively speaking.

We will concede that there is an element of this topic that has bearing on those who have experienced an abortion. By that I mean this: those who have found out after their wives or girlfriends had abortions without their knowledge or consent will have some similarities to those who have had miscarriages. However, it is vitally important to note that having an abortion, which takes a deliberate choice, is in no way similar to having a miscarriage. To the point that the principles and thoughts of this book overlap the struggles of a post-abortive situation, then that is great. However, this book is not nor will not address abortion as a deliberative, intentional act.

If you and your wife have been through a miscarriage, then this book is for you. If you think you are going through a miscarriage, this book is for you. If you know someone that has gone through a miscarriage, and you want to know how to help the person, then this book is for you and for that person as well. Or, if you simply want to understand miscarriage, this book is for you. Again, the fact that very little, if any, content has been published on this topic means that this book is unique in and of itself. To that end, I trust that this will provide some help for you and your wife.

Something else that is important to add is that this book is being written from a biblical worldview. This means that everything we discuss and talk about will be filtered through the lens of God's Word, the Bible. I concede that not everyone who reads this will share that same view. Throughout this book, you will see things addressed from the Biblical point of view. It is my prayer that if you do not have a Biblical worldview or if you do not have a relationship with Jesus Christ, that by the end of reading this book, you will.

So, guys, let's talk through this together, and let's begin to bring attention to the fact that miscarriage is a reality and that, although it affects the woman differently than the man, it still affects the man. Let's be blunt and real and, most importantly, let's have an honest conversation about what you are going through and how we can find hope and comfort from the Bible. Let's talk about how you deal with your emotions and how you lead your family through this silent pain. You are not alone! Men the world over have experienced miscarriage. Some have learned to deal with the miscarriage, and some have not. To those who have not learned how to deal with miscarriage, we desire to help.

I know that you may be reluctant to read, let alone to read a book on this topic. However, I believe that the journey you are about to embark on will bring insight, understanding, and even healing. Guys, you are not alone. I trust that this book will help you as much as it has helped me to write it. We have intentionally kept this as short and succinct as possible so that everyone who is interested in this topic can feel comfortable picking up this book and reading it. This is not intended to be an exhaustive treatise on the issue. It is intended, however, to give information, bring normalcy to discussions about miscarriage, and to give hope to all who read this book. To that end, I trust we will have accomplished our purpose.

CHAPTER 1

IT'S "JUST A MISCARRIAGE."

Death is difficult to deal with, no matter who has died. Death was certainly not part of the equation when God created Adam and Eve, so death is something that, even if we are prepared for it, we still struggle to cope with it and to process everything associated with it. Death crashes the party like an uninvited guest and causes more issues than we could ever have thought of. Death is expected by all but is anticipated by none. Yet, when death shows up in whatever form God allows, it is startling to us.

When death is experienced through the form of a miscarriage, it is even more difficult to process. Many times, you have no body to mourn, and you have no tangible expression of what you have lost. To be honest, the loss in miscarriage is a difficult experience. You have the sorrow associated with death but, because there is no body to mourn, you don't really know how to grieve properly. Sometimes, you think you should just move forward and chalk it up to life and try to act like nothing happened. Other times, you feel like you should sit in the ash heap of life and mourn silently in a secluded place. Death causes a plethora of emotions and responses.

The challenge with a miscarriage is that, unless someone has experienced one himself or herself, then the person will really struggle to know how to adequately help you. That is why some interesting stuff gets said to people when they have had a miscarriage. We will talk more about this in the next chapter. All throughout this book, we will share our story, not because we want to elicit sympathy or because we want to highlight ourselves in any way, but mostly because so few people discuss this topic, and there just aren't many other examples readily available to share. As we share our story, please understand that our sole intent is to give a frame of reference for a variety of situations and responses that may occur.

So here is our story. I hope by sharing this from a guy's perspective, that we can begin to draw some attention to helping men deal with the experience of a miscarriage.

A Little about Me, Just So You Are Aware…

I am not an overly expressive person emotionally. I never really have been and, to be quite honest, I am good with keeping things that way. This has it disadvantages, though. This means that in times of crisis or times of difficulty, I become stoic and methodical in how I respond to things. Maybe you can relate. My wife, although she benefits from it, is not a big fan of stoic, methodical Dave and, honestly, would like me to be a little bit more expressive in my emotions. I tend to think that at least one of us needs to be this way when it comes to our emotions and think clearly through things. At least that is what I keep telling myself. To me, talking about my feelings and expressing my emotions is not really high on my radar, so you can imagine writing a book about helping men deal with miscarriage is a bit of a surprise for my wife, for my friends and, yes, even for me.

For over twenty years, I served in pastoral ministry. This means that I had the responsibility to help couples through their times of loss during a miscarriage. From experience, I can tell you this: men and women handle this topic differently. Typically, men are not outwardly devastated nor are they really all that emotionally responsive to the miscarriage. This means that, often, the man's emotions and the man's viewpoint on miscarriage is overlooked. Many people will jump to help the woman, and rightly so; however, too many times, the man is left to process things on his own. To further complicate things, since men don't typically talk about the miscarriage, men typically resort to "stuffing" their feelings somewhere in a dark, forgotten corner.

Some men are very emotional, and a miscarriage can actually cause them deep emotional pain. They become distraught, depressed, and even feel hopeless in the process. The grief can become difficult for them to process and, if they aren't careful, the cold, sterile responses of other men can actually be a difficult thing for them in this process. As a man talking to other men who may be emotional, I would say this: "Grieve as God has designed you in your person to grieve." Do not, I repeat, do not let others tell you or mandate to you how you should respond or grieve in this process. If you need to go through the formal stages of grief, then feel free to do so.

As we share our story, one thing I wish I would have done, looking back, is to have taken more time to reflect on what happened to us. I didn't...and I think, in many ways, it would have been healthier for me to have responded differently. I could have been a better husband and, ultimately, a better father in the process. So, now, here I am nearly two decades later, working my way through this very personal topic.

So, Here Goes...

I am the youngest of four kids. My brother is nine-and-a-half years older than I am, and then I have a sister who is seven years older than I am and a sister who is five-and-a-half years older than I am. I believe that I was a surprise, but my parents say otherwise (Thank you to those of you who just said you agree that I was a surprise!). In many ways, I grew up as an only child. I was just starting eighth grade when my next oldest sibling went off to college. The oldest three kids were so far removed from me that even though they were around, we didn't have a lot in common given our age difference. I had friends that had large families, and, to some degree, I thought that it was cool that they all did stuff together and were close. However, when it came to me and the family Kimberly and I would have, I wasn't too keen on the notion of having a large family.

Kimberly and I met in college. It wasn't love at first sight or even second sight, but eventually we figured out that we actually liked each other, and we soon fell in love. As we dated, we discussed all aspects of the future children we would and would not have; I held firmly that one kid was about all I wanted to have. It wasn't that I didn't like kids; it is just that I didn't want to have a lot of them. Kimberly, well, she held out for six. Little did we know, at least for us, that trying to "plan" out your children is an endeavor in futility. However, at nineteen years of age, we thought we had most of life figured out.

We were married in August of 1998 when we were both twenty-one. We decided to use birth control that first year of marriage as I hadn't finished college yet and we weren't sure we were ready to start having a family. Almost immediately, Kimberly started to have some side effects of the birth control she was taking so, we started to look at other options. Over the course of the first two years, we had stopped using traditional birth control and Kimberly had gone on some medication that was throwing her hormones into a state of unpredictability. As a side note, this was a test of my ability to be sensitive—or at least my attempt to try to be sensitive. Most of the time, I failed.

On one occasion, I can remember displaying my great ability of being sensitive with Kimberly. She was in the kitchen of our little duplex making dinner, and I noticed that she was crying. I could not for the life of me figure out why she was crying (For the record, I don't always know how to handle when people cry.), so I grabbed her by both shoulders and asked her in a frustrated tone, "Isn't there a medicine you can take for this?" It should be noted that I am not necessarily advocating "drugging" people to get them to alter their emotional states but, in this case, it seemed like the best option. Fortunately for me, she found it humorous, and she responded in exasperation with the fact that she was on *that* medicine to help her with her hormones. This is the kind of interaction pastors don't talk about in pre-marital counseling!

It was shortly after that in November of 2000—almost two-and-a-half years after being married—that we found out we were pregnant for the first time. I was probably more in shock and disbelief than anything and seemed to kind of remember just living in a fog when it came to the reality of having a baby. It wasn't that I didn't want the baby; it was just that I really couldn't believe that I was actually going to be a dad. The feeling was surreal. Kimberly, on the other hand, was happy as a lark (not really sure how happy larks are, nor do I know if I have ever actually seen one, but you understand the expression.). She was thrilled with the fact that she was going to be a mommy, and she could hardly contain herself. From the outset, like many things in our relationship, we were dealing with reality in two different ways.

I was working for General Electric at the time in its gas turbine plant in Greenville, SC. Each day the older guys I worked with would give me a hard time about being a dad and all the responsibility and the challenges that I was about to experience. The workplace there was racially diverse, so I amused myself and the guys I worked with by throwing out a variety of names for the baby. Today, I probably would be in trouble with the HR department, but back then it was well received by everyone, regardless of the color of the person's skin. It was my way of dealing with the stress that I was going through, even though I didn't recognize it as stress and anxiety about being a dad.

On January 12, 2001, Kimberly had a routine appointment that she had to go to. At this point, she was about 12 weeks pregnant. Again, I was really not aware of all of the things she was going through with the pregnancy so, for me, it really wasn't a big deal that she was going to see the doctor.

Kimberly had been excited that we had found a Christian doctor to be her OB/GYN. This made her feel good about the fact that he valued life and he valued Christian morals. To be honest, I was happy with the fact that he was a Christian, but that is about as far as my analysis of the situation went.

About 1:00 in the afternoon, I received a phone call at work from Kimberly. When I answered, I was greeted by a woman who was in tears and who couldn't talk very clearly. In fact, I would describe her as being hysterical. As I tried to figure out what was going on, she finally got out the words that the doctor said that the baby was dead and that they wanted to take her into the next room and "take care of it." Naturally, I was in a bit of shock as I tried to process everything. I told her I would be right there and let my boss know, and I took off for the doctor's office.

My body was racing with adrenaline as I left work and got in my car. My heart and mind were out of control. I was trying to evaluate every type of response and what to do, not only for the situation, but also for Kimberly. Remember the fog I said I was in about the pregnancy? That fog seemed clearer to me than the situation I was now facing. Shock, fear, worry, concern, an unknown future, and denial would all adequately describe my feelings at the time. I had no way of making sense of anything as I raced to the doctor's office.

My mom spent nearly forty years as a nurse and, as was common whenever we had a medical question, she was the first one to call. So, on the way to the doctor's office, I called my mom and told her what was going on. My mom is a pretty rational and calm person, and this time was no different. She has an uncanny ability to deal with a crisis situation with amazing calm and clarity. This is probably why she made such a great nurse for so many years. She reminded me that the body is a unique creation and that if, in fact, the baby was dead, the body would handle it naturally. She reminded me that God was in control and that He would give wisdom to me and to Kimberly and to the doctors as they worked on her. I cannot tell you how much this calm, theologically rich reminder meant to me.

When I arrived at the doctor's office, I was taken back to the room where Kimberly was. Of course, tears were flowing (on her part), and this time I was smart enough not to make any stupid comments. I gave her a hug, and then we waited for the nurse to come in. When the nurse entered, she explained that the technician had not detected any heartbeat and that they presumed that the baby was dead. She explained that what they wanted to do was to take Kimberly into the next room and perform a D&E on her. A D&E is a term that stands for "dilate and evacuate." Basically, to put it bluntly, they stick a small vacuum inside the woman's uterus and remove the baby. We will talk more about this at the end of this chapter but, for now, let's just focus on the story.

At this point in the situation, there was so much shock and confusion. It was all moving so fast and was all very surreal. Just less than an hour before, we had been happily moving along with life and the pregnancy and then, like a forearm to the head from an MMA dude, we were blown over with this news that the baby was dead and not just that the baby was dead, they now wanted us to quickly make the decision to move into the next room and "take care of it." To say it was a blur would be as good of a description as I can give.

I composed myself and, thankfully, I was able to speak to the nurse. I informed the nurse that we preferred to wait and to see if, in fact, the baby was dead and, if it was, then we would let the body remove it naturally. I knew what my mom had said, and I believed that to be true. If the baby is, in fact, dead, then let's let the body naturally take its course. If the baby isn't dead, then let's not be hasty to circumvent the process. I am not sure how in agreement the nurse was with our saying that but, nonetheless, it was our decision, and she had no choice but to let us go home.

Once we got home, the reality of the events of the day began to sink in. Now, the suspense was a bit weird as we just had to wait to see what was going to happen. We called our pastor at church and let him know what was going on. Word spread among our church family and among our friends fairly quickly and, pretty soon, we had friends calling to express their concern. As much as I really appreciated the phone calls, I could tell that none of these people really knew what to say. That was fine, as I didn't really know what I wanted them to say anyway, and, plus, nothing had technically happened. Nothing was externally different than it was the day before. In a weird way, it was like a dream. You have this emotional crisis, make some decisions against the medical field experts' opinion, and you come home, and, if you hadn't been there yourself, you look at your wife and think that was all a dream. Literally, from an external physical perspective, nothing was any different on the afternoon of January 12 from what it had been on January 11.

The Waiting Begins…

When you are faced with a situation where you are forced to wait like this, it can be a very challenging process. Your life can't stop completely and, so, things go forward "like normal"; however, you have this weird processing going on in your head as you fathom the thought that something is going to happen at some point; you just don't know what exactly and when exactly. I have since had this same feeling as I have ministered to people in our church when they were told a family member had just a few days or hours to live. You know at some point things are going to deteriorate quickly, but you don't know when. The waiting is excruciating. The waiting in our situation was excruciating as well.

Kimberly went to work as normal on Monday, and I went to work as normal as well. The first day passed and nothing, then the second day and nothing, then the first week and still nothing. Kimberly wasn't experiencing any cramping or other indicators that something was wrong. It was a strange feeling as we just went about life as normal, all the while waiting with anticipation to see what was going to happen. We didn't know if anything was going to happen and, if it actually was going to happen, we had no idea *when* it was going to happen. You can almost get to a point where you begin to doubt if, in fact, the baby could possibly be dead. Your brain plays some crazy tricks on you as it tries to process everything.

The Day That Is Etched in My Mind…

That Friday started out like any other day. It had now been almost two weeks since Kimberly had been to the doctor. Thus far, nothing had happened at all or changed with Kimberly. I went to work and so did Kimberly. That night, we got home and decided that we would go grab some dinner at a local restaurant. As we were nearing the end of our meal, Kimberly began to complain of severe cramping. I think, at that moment, we both knew what was happening. However, neither one of us wanted to fully admit it or talk about it, but the reality was *it* had finally started. The indication that her body was, in fact, going to remove the body of our baby had started, and now we needed to get her the help that she needed.

We were not far from St. Francis Woman's Hospital in Greenville, SC. So, we got into the car and headed that way. I still didn't know what to expect to have happen. Probably adrenaline was kicking in—or maybe it was just anxiety and fear mixed together—but we walked into the lobby of the hospital, and we informed the nurse what was happening. The nurse that was there to admit us was gracious and kind, but she also had to inform us of some bad news. Typically, in a miscarriage where it is clear that the woman is at least a good portion of the way through the first trimester, the doctors will do a procedure known as a D&C. This is where the doctors go in and perform "minor" surgery to clean out all the tissue and all the parts of the baby that may be inside the uterus. Unfortunately for us, we were informed that surgery could not be performed for at least a few hours because Kimberly had just eaten dinner. I am not sure how much of that is necessary and how much is actually appropriate precaution. In my mind, the doctors wouldn't wait around like that if you had been in a car accident and needed emergency surgery. So, I was skeptical that they "HAD" to wait.

The nurse showed us to a room where we would need to wait until about 10:00 p.m. that evening before the doctor would be willing to perform the D&C. The nurse gave Kimberly the traditional hospital gown to put on, and she made sure that there was plenty of absorbent padding on the bed for her to sit on. And so, there we were in a little hospital room all by ourselves: Kimberly in her gown and me sitting in the uncomfortable chair in the room just waiting. It was a Friday night and, because it was a woman's hospital and not a traditional emergency care facility, it was relatively quiet where we were. In fact, it was so quiet that the nurse rarely checked on us. It was a weird kind of lonely.

It seems like it was about 8:00 p.m. or so when Kimberly's cramps worsened. Her body then began to miscarry the baby. She began to hemorrhage blood and tissue in large clots. The padding on the bed quickly became soaked in blood. I ran down the hall looking for a nurse and was told one would be in very shortly. I returned to the room to find Kimberly sobbing as she continued to hemorrhage. That moment that I walked back into the room has been one of the worst moments in my life. At that moment in time, I was angry. I was angry because of what my wife was going through, and I was angry that the doctor "couldn't do the surgery" when we arrived and, to be honest, I was probably angry that now I was having to deal with something that made me feel totally helpless. My wife was bleeding profusely on the table, and we were all by ourselves. On the table were clumps of blood and bodily tissue, and it was bad, really, really bad! Kimberly was sitting in the midst of our baby's remains and sobbing, and I didn't have a clue how to help the situation.

The nurse arrived soon after that, and she made a statement that I will never forget. She said, "Oh, yep, she is just having a miscarriage." Now, I do understand, having a mom who was a nurse, that it is easy for medical personnel to deal with things so much that it just becomes second nature, and they don't even think about things the way other non-medical people think about things. It really can happen in any profession. It can happen as a pastor. "Oh, yep, they are just getting a divorce" or "Oh, yep, he died last night." We deal with things so regularly that the shock of the situation actually wears off and we don't even think about the shock that the people we are dealing with are going through. I believe that that is what happened with this nurse. For her, this was an average day at the hospital. There was blood and there were tears, and it was all just another day at the hospital.

For me, however, it was an offensive and confusing statement. To me, "Oh, yep, she is just having a miscarriage" was like saying, "The car needs gas" or "Can you take the dog for a walk?" To me, as I sat trying to hold and comfort my wife as best as I knew as her body violently removed the bodily tissue of our baby, I was traumatized. So, to hear this statement made me think, "Pull it together, Deets. This isn't that big of deal; it happens all of the time." I think, at that moment, I began to deal with our miscarriage in a way that would have said, "Buck up dude. Emotions are for sissies!" For me, that was the moment when I seriously suppressed any emotional consideration of difficulty regarding the miscarriage and regarding the events that happened. We will talk later about why that isn't a good response.

The nurse informed us that now that Kimberly had had the miscarriage, the doctor could go in and perform the

D&C. The nurse sent me out of the room and prepared Kimberly for surgery. The surgery itself lasted about 25-30 minutes. Once she was in recovery, the doctor came out to talk to me about what he had done and what to expect. It was about 11:00 p.m.. Nothing he said was shocking or earth shattering. Even though he was very matter of fact, he was caring and sensitive about the situation as well. After all, this was her Christian OB/GYN that performed the surgery. He was gracious and he was kind and he certainly cared for Kimberly and for me. What happened next, I am not sure I would do again, but for sake of our story, I will share this part as well.

I Felt Like It Needed to Be Said...

Once the surgery was completed, and the doctor had come to meet me in the waiting room, he asked if there was anything else that I needed. At the time I felt very compelled to talk to him. I am not necessarily inclined to speak up and say something to someone unless it really strikes a wrong chord in me. In this case, I knew this was something that I needed to talk to him about. I expressed my concern with how quickly the nurse in his office had wanted to "just go next door and take care of it." I told him that since we believe that life begins at conception, her comment was a rather matter-of-fact and— to be quite honest—rash decision given that the body will take care of the miscarriage naturally. I expressed to him that he, being a believer and strong supporter of life, would do well to make some changes with his practice (Yes, I concede I was a twenty-four-year-old kid telling a seasoned MD what to do.). He thanked me for my comments and said he would definitely look at things in his office.

I don't want to sound like I had it all together when I was talking with the doctor. Personally, I feel as though an opportunity presented itself and I took advantage of the situation and responded, for once, to the prompting of God to talk to him. In hindsight, I may not have been as gracious as I should have been, but it was what I said. We will discuss some more of this type of response later.

Kimberly was released from the hospital, and we stopped at Walgreen's on the way home to pick up her pain meds and headed for our little duplex of a house. I would say that what I felt like at that time was like a dog who had its tail between its legs, cowering for cover in the darkness. I felt defeated and helpless and probably just weird. Words like, "confused," "dazed," and "in shock" all would probably describe how I felt at the time. In a strange way, I felt like my manhood (Can you actually produce a child?) had been challenged, and my manhood forgot to show up to the game!

We had gone through a miscarriage, but for us, it wouldn't be the last. We would have many more challenges in the years to come. However, this first experience of a miscarriage had smacked us pretty good. It was kind of like being sucker-punched. You didn't even have a chance to fight back. It kicked your butt when you weren't looking and then walked off like a punk leaving you in the hallway after stealing your lunch money! We wandered home at 1:00 a.m. on a Saturday morning, dazed and confused.

A Take Away…

Guys, let me talk bluntly to you. The baby that your wife is carrying is yours as much as hers. Virtually everyone in the world today is screaming that this is the *woman's* body, the *woman's* decision, and the *woman's* right to do with it as she wills. Even though we aren't talking about your wife having an abortion, if you aren't aware, the doctor she visits may handle things like our Christian doctor did: "Take her in the next room and (in essence) perform a proactive procedure to remove the baby." What is discussed in the next few paragraphs is complicated, difficult, and must be handled with the utmost sensitivity.

Here's the deal: on one hand, I will give you the same advice my mom gave me. The body is uniquely designed to naturally remove the baby if, in fact, it is dead. Do not believe the statement that says we have to go right now and suck it out. There are ample stories of times when the doctors were wrong and what they thought was a dead baby was, in fact, not a dead baby. Be courageous and stand for life. If possible, try to let her body take care of things as God has designed. Is it difficult? Yes! However, I cannot tell you how thankful I am that we did not rush Kimberly into the next room to do a D&E.

On the other hand, let me also state something else just as clearly. (And, lest you think I am two-faced, let me state that this situation requires a tremendous amount of wisdom and discernment.). From a medical perspective, you need to know this. It is sometimes okay to wait and let the body take care of what is going on in the time frame the body needs. However, there are times where that can be a danger to the mother, and other options must be considered. Depending on the length of time the provider thinks the baby passed away before it was found can make a big difference in how they determine the best way to proceed.

There are times when waiting for too long can cause sepsis and far more life-threatening issues, such as DIC. Disseminated intravascular coagulation (DIC) is a condition in which blood clots form throughout the body, blocking small blood vessels. This condition is complicated and rare, but it does happen, and it is not pretty. Absolutely every single available option, along with benefits and risks of those options, should be discussed so that the patient and spouse can make an informed decision of what they want the next step to be, and it should be done so in a manner that gives them time to digest the information given and to grieve in whatever manner they need to.

The fact of the matter is that two different people could be reading this book and have two completely different responses of what to do. What we have tried to present here is both options. There is not necessarily a right or wrong answer for everyone. Each situation and each person are different. You should have the freedom to make the choice, like we did, to wait. At the same time, you should have the freedom to have a real, meaningful conversation with your medical provider about all of the risks and issues you may experience by waiting. If, after discussing the situation with your doctor, you feel it is wise to take care of the baby at that moment in time, you should feel the freedom to do that.

I am also aware that I may be speaking to people who are on the backside of a situation like this, and maybe you had a D&E. You made the decision to "go into the next room." What now? As you read this book, you may be filled with so much guilt that you just cannot bear to read further. I want to assure you that God loves you just as much today as He did the day you made the decision to have the D&E. He also is the

God of grace and mercy, and I do not believe for one minute that God looks at you, as a couple, and holds this against you in some way. You know who wants to hold this against you? The Evil One wants to hold this against you and remind you of this. Friends and family may hold this against you, but that is them and not God. Please do not allow yourself to be overtaken with guilt if you have done this. We will address some more aspects of dealing with this in the chapters to come.

This is one of the most difficult, most sensitive parts of the miscarriage process. When God allows you to "be in charge" of the situation, if you will, and make a decision. Every decision comes with consequences. Our decision came with consequences. Please know this: God loves you. He is there for you. He wants to lavish His grace on you. You can trust Him to give you the wisdom you need in order to make the decision He desires you to make.

I would suggest that you learn from the situation in which you may have made a quick decision, prepare for it if it happens again, and rest in the gracious arms of Jesus. He loves you and cares more for you than you will ever know. I trust that you will be able to effectively deal with whatever guilt you may be experiencing in this process. The unfortunate reality is that for some of you reading this book, this idea hits far too close to home. If that is the case, I would strongly urge you to get help. See a Biblical counselor or seek help from a pastor who can help you deal with the past decisions you have made that now clutter your mind with regret.

CHAPTER 2

IT HAPPENS TO A LOT OF PEOPLE.

What I soon realized after our first miscarriage was that people didn't really know what to do or say. Most women who had had a miscarriage were able to comfort Kimberly and provide some sense of encouragement. However, guys just didn't talk about this stuff. I remember the exception to this was my best friend Steve, who called me to talk about it and asked me lots of questions about it but, outside of that, guys just didn't know what to say or do. This practice really encourages guys with the idea of pushing it away and acting like it didn't happen. You already don't want to talk about it and then, to complicate the matter, the conversations you wind up having about miscarriage as a guy gets awkward really fast.

However, even though many did not know what to say and, honestly, just wanted to be there to show their love and support, there were some people that did want to make comments about the miscarriage. This occurred more to

Kimberly than to me, but, nonetheless, they were trying to help, I am sure, but in the process of trying to help, in some cases, they actually made things worse. As you think through the process of dealing with a miscarriage, you also have to be aware that there are things that will be said to you that will cause you to take a step back. My goal in this section is not to be disparaging of these people, but rather to help you, first of all, not be someone who says these types of things to others but, second, to know how to deal with and process these statements.

I would categorize these types of people into the following four different statements below. I think it is important to know some of the things that may be said to you or to your wife that warrant a proper response I will be honest: some of this stuff may make you want to punch someone in the face. However, you have the obligation to respond appropriately to people when they respond inappropriately to you. I do believe that most people are trying to help. However, I also believe that age-old statement my mom said to me many times, "If you don't have anything nice to say, or don't know what to say, don't say anything at all" is fitting! Either way, it is helpful to be able to be prepared for what may come your way.

God Is Judging You!

In some belief systems, even among those who would claim to be evangelical Christians, there is the idea that God is out to get you. So, any trial or difficulty that arises is automatically chalked up to God's judgment in your life for something. You may or may not know what you did, but the fact of the matter is that, at least to these people, if you face a trial of some kind, it is because God is judging you. Dealing with these types of people is not only aggravating, but it is, to be honest, hard to be nice when people say insensitive things. Such was the case with a "friend" that contacted Kimberly shortly after one of our miscarriages.

After the multiple miscarriages we had had, Kimberly's friend contacted her via email to let Kimberly know that the miscarriage(s) she was experiencing was a sign of God's judgment. This person insisted that God was judging or cursing Kimberly in some capacity for some reason. It is difficult for me to process the insensitivity of someone who would contact someone else during their pain to inform them of this God-given "knowledge". However, as was our Kimberly's situation, this is exactly what happened.

This person had known Kimberly when they were younger, and she herself had been able to have multiple successful pregnancies without incident. In many regards, we would say, "Congratulations, and we are happy for you!" However, with this particular person and her particular view of children, you may need to know something about her first. Here is the premise with her belief: if you have lots of children and successful pregnancies, then God is heaping blessings on you. However, if you do not have children or you have difficulty with pregnancies, then you must be doing something wrong, and God needs to punish you for that. Before you totally freak out, let me explain the "logic."

Okay, so for this one, you will need to find a Bible and look at Psalms 127:3-5. In case you don't have access to a Bible right now, let me share with you what this says:

3   Behold, children are a heritage from the LORD, the fruit of the womb a reward.

4   Like arrows in the hand of a warrior are the children of one's youth.

5   Blessed is the man who fills his quiver with them! He shall not be put to shame when he speaks with his enemies in the gate.

I know some of you are already connecting the dots on this one. However, let me just work our way through this. Because, if you happen to come across someone who thinks the way Kimberly's friend thinks, you should be able to respond with a Biblically accurate response.

The position held by this woman is this: if the Bible says, *"If this happens, this is a blessing from God,"* then the opposite must be true, which would be as follows: *"If this does not happen, then this a sign of God judging you."* I would call it the Law of Converse Principles. It is faulty Biblical logic and understanding, but, nonetheless, it exists. So, in this case, to those who think this way, if God says that having children is a blessing and the fruit of the womb is a reward, then the opposite must be true, at least in their minds. To these people, not being able to have children must be a sign of God's judgment, and not having a fruitful womb is a sign of God, in essence, cursing you. This is a horrible interpretation of Scripture!

This theological argument can show up in groups that have connections with a legalistic group within the Independent Fundamental Baptist circles or even Pentecostal/Charismatic circles. Many of these people take these Old Testament passages as always applicable to all people at all times and, therefore, take the converse of these statements as always applicable to all people at all times as well. Is having children a sign of God's blessing? Sure. Is not having children a sign of failure, a curse or judgment from God? No! Here's why. The fall of mankind into sin at the beginning through Adam caused there to be consequences that fell upon all of mankind. Among those consequences is not just pain in childbirth, as we see in Genesis 3, but also complications within childbearing among a host of other issues. So, people struggle with infertility and people struggle with physical complications that lead to miscarriage. So, to say that if your wife has a miscarriage, that this must mean that she is being judged by God or cursed by God is to grossly misinterpret Scripture. Guys, listen, do not allow anyone to tell your wife that nonsense. And if someone does tell her that, help her to understand that if she has a miscarriage, it isn't because God is mad at her and is trying to punish her.

We can see this at play in I Samuel with the story of Hannah. Hannah had one desire, and that was that God would bless her with a child. There is no indication in Scripture that Hannah had somehow been unfaithful to God or that she was facing consequences as a result of some sin she had committed. In fact, we see Hannah as a faithful, godly woman who simply begged God for the blessing of a child. Her desire was for a child. We know from I Samuel that God eventually blessed her with a child, which, miraculously, she gave back in service to God. God was faithful to Hannah when she could not have children, and God was faithful to Hannah after she had a child.

Let me say something to you at this point: just because you and your wife have struggled to have children, whether through lack of an ability to conceive or through struggles with miscarriage, please know that God is not judging you, nor is He "out to get you." Be patient, be faithful, be trusting and allow God in His sovereign will to accomplish His plan in your life. Everything that happens to us is for our good and for His glory. We trust the immutability of God (meaning He cannot change). Therefore, God's inability to change means that He will never be any more good than He is today, nor any less good than He is today. He is perfectly in control, and He will give you a child when He desires to give you a child. Please do not allow a statement like that of "God is judging you" to have bearing on your life. Be gracious in your response and, yet, at the same time be encouraged through the word of God.

You Are Better off Not Having Had It!

Kimberly's due date for the first baby we lost was actually set for July 28, 2001. As God would see fit, I had been able to transfer to Ft. Wayne, Indiana, to work in a medical malpractice insurance office. I had worked for General Electric in Greenville, and now I would be working for General Electric in Ft. Wayne. We had moved to the area to help a small church. As it worked out, we had just arrived in the area, and the Pastor's wife had decided to take Kimberly out for lunch to welcome her to the area.

While the two ladies were at lunch, Kimberly mentioned that that day was a special day as it would have been the due date of our baby. The pastor's wife responded, "You know what? It is probably good you didn't have the baby anyway with the move and everything. It would have been a lot of extra hassle to have a newborn and trying to do the move. You are better off not having had it." Now, I have made it clear that I am not super-sensitive and emotional, but even I know this is not something that should have been said.

Again, I know that this woman was just "trying to help." She obviously wanted Kimberly to think about how stressful the move had been and to think about how much more stressful it would have been for us to have a newborn baby and then to realize how grateful she should be in the situation at the time. I want to believe with all of my heart that she literally did not believe that the baby's life mattered so little that we would be happy that we had the miscarriage so that our lives would not be so stressful. I do believe she was really trying to help, but making this kind of statement on a day like this was very hurtful.

However, the more that you process something like this, the more you realize that no gracious person would say something like this to someone who lost a child after birth. For instance, let's imagine that someone you know has a seventeen-year-old kid and six weeks prior to his graduation from high school as he excitedly receives his acceptance letter to his chosen university and is anticipating what lies ahead of him, he is suddenly killed in a car accident. Let's say that it is now the first of September of that year, and you are having lunch with the people who lost their child in the car accident a few months prior. Imagine that, as they are talking about some challenges that they are going through in life unrelated to the death of their child, they off-handedly mention to you that today would have been their child's first day of college. There is literally no way that you would be inconsiderate enough to say to that person, "You know what? It is probably good that your child died because you wouldn't want the added stress of a college bill on top of everything else. You are better off not having your child anymore."

Why things like this are deemed appropriate to say to people who have a miscarriage I will never know. I believe that at the heart of it is the idea that that the loss of that baby is minimal, especially in comparison to the loss of someone outside of the womb. To a degree, this is true. No one who has had a miscarriage would argue that it is just as emotionally difficult to lose a baby at six weeks or even twelve weeks in the womb as it is to lose a good friend or family member who has lived twenty or thirty or more years. I do not believe anyone would argue for that. However, people who are insensitive to the hurt and the consequences of a miscarriage will definitely try to minimize your pain, your hurt, and your emotional responses during a miscarriage. And, in trying to minimize your pain or your hurt or, in some cases, "just trying to help," they will wind up causing more damage and more hurt.

So how do we respond to something like this? There is a particular passage of Scripture that comes to mind as we think through this type of scenario. I am going to assume that the person who said these things to Kimberly or, in your case, to you or your wife is not actually trying to hurt you but rather, in extreme ignorance, is trying to minimize what you went through in order to help. So, I would like us to consider a passage in the book of Proverbs—Proverbs 27:17:

[17] Iron sharpens iron, and one man sharpens another.

Here is one way I believe you can handle this situation. You may not be able to address it at the exact moment someone says something like this to you, but you need to address it fairly quickly. You can say something like this: "When you say we would be better off not having had the baby due to the other stresses of life, I understand to a degree what you mean, but I feel it really distorts the value that God places on life, whether in the womb or outside of the womb. And, to be transparent, it really hurts to think about having to agree with you that we would not have wanted the baby to live because nothing could be farther from the truth. Yes, life would have had more stress if we did have the baby to take care of right now, but that does not in any way negate our love for and desire to have had our baby make it to full-term and be able to be a part of our lives. And, if the baby would have lived and been born now, we would have trusted God to give us the grace and strength to take care of it, and we know He would have done that for us." I trust that, if you did that, the person who made the original statement would immediately realize the hurt he or she caused.

Again, we must be reminded of the Biblical principle of speaking the truth in love. We must show grace, even when grace has not necessarily been extended to us. This is difficult to do at times but, with God's help, we can show a Christ-like response to others in the midst of these challenging situations. I am certain that there will come a point in your life where you will have to deal with this kind of response. In that situation, I pray that you can show God's grace to that individual.

It Happens to a lot of People!

A third statement that we heard was based on the fact that "it happens to a lot of people." I would call this a desire for people to get you to reflect on the fact that this is common, that you are not alone, and that there wasn't much you could do about it, so don't think about it, and just move on. Of all the things that could be said to you, this response is not too difficult to hear; however, if you are needing some encouragement or emotional support or someone just to truly ask you about what you just went through, then this response will not facilitate that.

Here's the deal with this response. Do not take it personally if people tell you this. In other words, it isn't that they don't care about you or that they don't want to help you. This response typically comes from people who have not had a miscarriage or from people who may have known people who had a miscarriage but are not aware of the emotional challenges of having a miscarriage. However, what you do need to do is to make sure that you find your satisfaction and sufficiency in Jesus Christ. Is it nice to have people care about you? Absolutely! Is it nice to have people ask you about what you experienced and how you are doing and what did you feel? Absolutely! However, it is Christ and Christ alone who satisfies. Instead of fuming over someone not asking you questions you wanted to be asked, turn to Christ to find your satisfaction.

The fact that miscarriage happens to a lot of people should also remind you that you are not alone. What we have learned through this process is that many of our friends went through miscarriage at some point in their lives and that, for the most part, we had no idea. Because no one talks about this issue, it is easy for us to think that we are in some unique group with a few other people in the world. The reality is that virtually everyone has either been through a miscarriage or knows someone who has. So, yes, the fact that it happens to a lot of people can be a bit deflating but, on the other hand, it should inform us that we certainly are not alone. Again, be gracious in your response and recognize the perspective of the person saying this to you.

You Just Need to Get Back on the Horse!

The final comment was one that I actually received. It came from the group of guys I worked with at the time of our first miscarriage. To be honest, these guys were pretty empathetic to what we were going through and, though most did not have a relationship with Christ at all, they certainly were not lacking in a desire to console me. Two guys in particular that I worked with were Charlie and Randy. They both could have been old enough to be my dad, and I think they actually took the news pretty hard. The group I worked with had formed a pretty good relationship, and we had had a lot of fun joking around about different names for the baby. So, when I let them know that we had had a miscarriage, they were saddened by the news.

Most of the guys I worked with didn't have much to say about it as far as words of wisdom to me or consoling statements. I knew they cared, and I knew they hated that we were going through this. I remember on the night I had let them all know that we had lost the baby, Charlie pulled me aside from the rest of the group and told me, "You just need to get back on the horse." Of course, that expression was coming from an old-time kind of Southern boy. There was nothing derogatory at all that was meant by that statement; he was just simply trying to let me know that these things happen and that you move on, and you just keep at it.

It is ironic to me that an unsaved guy would have a better response than some of our saved friends did with the whole situation. And, yes, I did need to be able to move on, and I did need to be able to help Kimberly as we struggled through these things together. However, here is a bit of the danger in all of this. If we just simply "get back on the horse," as Charlie would say, and never talk about these things, we are in danger of carrying some emotional baggage with us as we go through life. I think that Kimberly and I were able to talk about some of these things at the time, but there would come a moment in the future where we would have to make some decisions regarding our future in this area. Even though we talked, I don't think we knew what all to talk about.

There are certainly a number of other things that could be said and, in fact, have been said to people who have had miscarriages. No matter what, know that you are not alone, neither in actually having a miscarriage nor in having people say things to you in the midst of your dealing with a miscarriage. You may have to endure some difficult statements from so-called friends.

So here are some things to consider discussing as a couple, especially if you have had any number of miscarriages:

1. *You need to discuss how serious you both are in having children.* If there is a difference between the two of you on this matter, you must talk about this. If one of you is bent on having children no matter what and the other of you is indifferent or opposed to having children no matter what, there will be a wedge that can eventually begin to develop between the two of you and your relationship. In our case, I was not as committed to having children as Kimberly was, and that was something that eventually had to be discussed.

Fortunately, for us, we were able to address things before they became bigger issues.

2. *You need to discuss what costs you are willing to pay in order to have children.* This is not just financial, but it is also physical and emotional as well. If you decide to pursue medical treatment or you decide to adopt, there are going to be financial commitments that you are agreeing to. Both of you must be willing to agree to the financial costs that potentially will be involved in this process.

    If you decide that you are going to go through with medical treatment, or you are going to try to adopt, or you are just going to "call it quits," then you have to understand that there will be an emotional and physical cost that both of you have to be willing to "pay." You have to talk about this, and you both have to be willing to find a consensus on this.

3. *You need to discuss if and when your wife is ready for sex again.* I say your wife because we know that, as a general rule, men are always ready for sex. However, if your wife has had a miscarriage, you need to ask her or at least have her communicate with you in some capacity, when she is ready both physically and emotionally to have sex. I think as men we can comprehend that she may not be ready physically, but you need to understand that, as a woman, your wife may not be ready emotionally to have sex because of what it represents and because of what she just went through. Men, be patient and communicative with her.

4. *You need to discuss the emotional toll each of you has gone through every time you have a miscarriage.* Every time you have a miscarriage, you need to talk about how you both are doing, what you are feeling, how you are dealing with things, and so on. Men, I am saying this as someone who acknowledges that he is not super-emotional and "touchy-feely"; however, I am telling you that you need to talk with your wife about the emotional toll this miscarriage has had on both of you.

    You may not be able to articulate everything well, and you may not be able to even understand everything. However, setting aside time to be intentional in communicating about what you are thinking and feeling will be invaluable to you and to your relationship with your wife.

We will get into some of these discussions a bit in the next chapter but, before you just "get back on the horse," make sure you have had time to talk through these things with each other. You may not know everything to ask or say, but just talking together will help you both understand where each other are.

How we respond says a lot about us. I would say that our responses should be gracious and appropriate. They need to be intentional responses, which not only express how we may be feeling, but also are opportunities used to point people to Jesus Christ and to make sure that we do our part to give Him honor. Certainly, these four statements are not the only ones that you may encounter, but I hope that by working ourselves through each of these you have seen how you might be able to respond graciously and appropriately to people.

Let me explain it a different way: God cares more about the relationship between you and your wife than He does about which decision you have made regarding what you will do in the future regarding children. God desires that your relationship is focused on Him and focused on being right with each other. Above anything else you could value or hold dear; this is something you need to value and hold dear. Amidst all of the other challenges you face in life, you need to ensure that you and your wife have a relationship that glorifies God.

A Take Away...

Guys, the one person you should care about most in this entire process is your wife. You will have people telling you a lot of different things. There will be people telling your wife a lot of different things. There will be plenty of things that could potentially drive a wedge between you and your wife. Do not let that happen! Make sure that you both have regular relationship checks to make sure you are both doing okay and both handling the situation properly. At the end of the day, you are not married to your mom or your friend at work or your childhood friend, you are married to your wife and, right now, the two of you are going through a unique situation together. Focus on her and your relationship with her. This may not always be easy to do given some of the emotions and hormones that can be involved in the process of a miscarriage, but you need to be quick to protect your relationship with your wife.

CHAPTER 3

IT'S DIFFERENT BUT THE SAME:
DEALING WITH EACH OTHER IN LOSS

Guys, I will just shoot really straight with you: when it comes to miscarriage, you have no perceived struggles with the emotional side of dealing with it. By that, I mean this: the vast majority of people will be concerned about your wife. How is she doing physically? How is she doing emotionally? Even, how is she doing spiritually? However, very few people, if any, including even your wife potentially, will even think about asking you about how you are doing. It isn't that your wife doesn't love you or doesn't care about you. It is just that miscarriage affects men and women so differently that rarely will people know what to do with you.

You should not be offended by this reality. If anything, this reality, along with what we are discussing in this book, should give us hope that maybe we can play a small part in changing the reality. As we think through this section, we will have a chance to help one another relationally. This is one of the most important aspects of dealing with a miscarriage. Whether we want to admit it or not, relational issues between a husband and wife, due to miscarriage, have been the cause of some marriages breaking apart. So, let's take a few minutes and talk about how you and your wife can help each other in this process of dealing with a miscarriage.

Guys, What Can You Do for Her?

Guys, we will start with you, as you will set the tone for how things will heal in your family after a miscarriage. There are so many emotions that will be swirling around your wife that you need to be aware of and that you need to be able to help her with. It is important to be sensitive and caring during this time. Even though you may not understand everything that she is going through, here are some basic, practical things you can do for your wife during this time.

So, here goes guys. This list is not a full list of everything you can and should do, but it will at least get you started.

Love Her.

The Bible talks about the type of love that men are to have for their wives. It is called a "self-sacrificing love" (see Ephesians 5:22-33). In other words, it sacrifices its own desires, or wants (in this case the man's desires and wants), in order to provide for and meet the needs of the wife. There will be a variety of emotional, physical, spiritual and, yes, even sexual needs that your wife will have during this time. It is your goal to love her unconditionally, despite what she may act like or how you may feel about the situation.

So, what exactly does this look like? This means that you may not understand why she started to cry randomly, why she is struggling with her self-image, or why she is angry or frustrated with you for no apparent reason, but you still love her. You still go out of your way to show love to her in the best way you know how. It means that even if she is acting in a way that makes you shake your head with absolute frustration because you can't seem to figure her out, you still love her. It means you spend time with her, it means you do the dishes or cook dinner, it means you buy her flowers, and it means you write her a note of encouragement. Whatever it is that makes her feel loved, you do it because it is during this time following a miscarriage that your wife will be going through more emotions and struggles than *she* even knows what to do with.

One of the greatest things you can do as a man, as a husband, is to show unconditional love to your wife. This is seen in the bedroom as well. One of the most significant ways you can show this kind of self-sacrificing love is by being patient and selfless when it comes to sex. Make sure that you seek to meet *her* emotional needs and *her* spiritual and physical needs first. There may be a desire for intimacy that will help her (cuddling, kissing etc. without an expectation of sex). This will not only allow you to build a better relationship with her, but it will allow you to help her through the emotional, spiritual, and even physical minefield that she is navigating as she goes through the miscarriage and the aftermath. This is not always easy to do, but it is one of the most important things you can and must do for your wife. In the long run, this will speak volumes to her as you both navigate the emotions involved in a miscarriage. Too many guys are impatient with their wives, and this is detrimental to their relationship.

Men, it is simple to say, love her, and yet, it is one of the most difficult things we must do as husbands. As you engage your wife in the process of dealing with miscarriage, the first thing you need to do is to love her. If you do not do anything else, do this. Loving your wife in the way that God intended a husband to love his wife will lead to the fulfillment of these other suggestions.

Hold Her.

Now, there needs to be an asterisk to this one; if for some reason your wife hates to be held, then don't do this one. However, for the 99.99% rest of you, this one will be applicable. One of the greatest things you can do for your wife to assure her that everything is going to be okay is to just hold her. Hold her after dinner while you sit on the couch. Hold her in bed as you drift off to sleep. Hold her without the expectation of sex. Hold her hand, wrap your arm around her, sit behind her, and hold her. Wherever and whenever you can hold her, then hold her. This is one of the most effective ways of communicating love and security to your wife during this time.

Again, guys don't understand a lot if any of what she is going through emotionally, physically, or spiritually. So, one of the best things you can do is just hold her. Be there for her to provide a tangible expression of love and comfort to her. You do not have to necessarily understand everything that she is going through or that she may say to you, but something that will help her feel safe and secure and feel like everything will be okay is for you to hold her and be a source of strength for her. This security for her will be instrumental in helping her be ready to talk with you and to confide emotionally in you.

Again, this is not for some ulterior motive for you to get sex, but rather it is simply to comfort and to help her. When you meet her needs emotionally without expectations in return, you will be able to not only assure her of your love for her, but you will also be able to help her get back to the emotional state she needs to be in.

Listen to Her.

Guys, let's just admit it right here: we aren't good at listening. At least most of us aren't. We have a hard time multitasking, and we all know that, if the game is on, listening just isn't going to happen. So, here's the deal. I would strongly encourage you to turn off the radio, the TV, the computer, the phone, or whatever device you may have, and give your wife your undivided attention and ask her about what she is going through. It might confuse you, it might gross you out, it might do a lot of things to you, but the one thing it will do for you is that it will greatly enhance your relationship with your wife.

The one thing your wife needs right now is for her best friend and life partner (That's you, by the way!) to be there for her to listen to her. So, go ahead, ask her about what she is feeling. Ask her about what she is afraid of. Ask her how her pain is. Ask her about what she is struggling with when it comes to God right now. Ask her about what she fears. Or maybe don't ask her anything, but just tell her you are there for her and whatever she wants to talk about and assure her that you want to listen. And then, wait for it...actually *listen* to her. Don't give her advice, don't give her suggestions, and don't give her anything other than your attentive ear. If she asks for advice, counsel, or suggestions, then by all means give it to her with grace and tact, but the most important thing you can do emotionally for her is to listen to her. Let her know that you care by how engaged you are in listening to her.

This is probably one of the most difficult and uncomfortable things for you as a guy to do. However, you will never regret taking the time to love your wife in this way. I can tell you from experience as someone who did not do this that you will miss out on significant emotional, spiritual, and even physical, intimate connections to your wife if you fail to do this for her. Guys, this is an area where we all need to grow. We must listen to understand and not just simply to respond.

Assure Her.

Guys, our wives are tough girls. I am not just talking about what they have just gone through with the miscarriage but, in general, they are tough. Here is where I struggle in this area. I assume that since Kimberly is a tough girl that she doesn't need reassurance at times. It is easy for me to think of her emotionally like she is a guy. She is going to tough it up and get through it. Guys generally don't need a good cry and a hug. Women, on the other hand, though they may be tough as nails, still need assurance. They need to know things are okay and are going to be okay. This is the role that we as men can excel at, assuming we realize this sooner rather than later.

So, what can you assure her of? Assure her that you love her no matter what. Sometimes the woman will take it personally that she is somehow responsible for the miscarriage. She needs you to reassure her that, no matter what happens, you do and always will love her. Assure her that you aren't mad at her. Again, it is often the case that the wife will assume the blame for the miscarriage. She will think and believe that she should have done something different. She should not have exercised, or eaten something, or done that much physical work, or whatever. The emotions of the situation will often convince your wife that she is at fault and that you are mad at her for somehow messing things up. Nothing, and I mean nothing, could be further from the truth. What your wife needs is for you to assure her that it is not her fault and that in no way are you angry, irritated, or upset with her.

You can also assure her that you want to be intimate again with her. The self-esteem of a woman can take a severe blow when she has a miscarriage. This can affect your sex life. I know for guys this is hard to imagine because there is little, if anything, that affects sex for us. However, your wife needs you to assure her that when she is ready (Can I just repeat that again? When *she* is ready), you can't wait to be intimate with her again. Encourage her with the fact that she is beautiful and sexy and that you find her attractive and that you want to share intimate time with her. She needs that reassurance. Finally, assure her that there is nothing wrong with her. Your wife will be tempted to think that she is weird or that she has something wrong with her. Now, granted, there may be medical/physical type issues that are going on in your wife's body, but this is in no way a reflection of her. You need to assure her that she isn't some weird statistic or that no one else could possibly have had a miscarriage except for her. She needs to hear from you and be reassured from you that she is okay.

Pray for and with Her.

Guys don't often like to discuss deep spiritual things. I am not sure why that is but, as a general rule, guys shy away from that stuff at times. Well, the last two suggestions are going to be spiritual. If you aren't a spiritual person or if you do not normally engage in spiritual/church things, then this section may be somewhat confusing for you. However, if you are a spiritually-minded guy, then I trust this will be an encouragement for you.

Guys, you need to pray for your wife. I know you may say that you don't know what to pray for her about. So let me give you a few suggestions of how you can pray for her.

1. *Pray that she recovers physically.* Your wife has, in essence, gone through a delivery of a child. She bled a lot and, therefore, she has the potential for infection. She has the potential for other physical side effects. So, pray for her and her physical recovery. Pray that she would be able to heal appropriately and that she would not have any repercussions from the miscarriage. Pray that she has the physical strength necessary to be able to return to normal activities. Pray that she would not have any lingering physical challenges as she heals.

2. *Pray that she recovers emotionally.* Again, I know you will say that you do not understand all of the emotions. I remember Kimberly crying at random times and, at times, I thought we should have been well beyond the immediate issues of the miscarriage. It is important for you to be sensitive to these situations and to be careful in how you interact and respond to her.

Pray that your wife would be able to heal emotionally. Pray that you would be able to be there for her to encourage her and pray that God would give you wisdom to know what to say and what to do. Pray that God would provide a good support system of girlfriends for your wife that she can confide in and that she can talk to.

3. *Pray that she recovers spiritually.* One of the greatest attacks on your wife spiritually will occur during a miscarriage. Is God in control? Why did He allow this to happen to me? Can I trust Him that He really loves me? Is God judging me? The list of "what if" type questions can go on and on. You need to pray for your wife, and let's go a step further. Dude, you need to lead your wife spiritually all of the time, but especially, I repeat, especially during this time. Get your head away from your phone or away from the TV and spend time engaging with your wife on a spiritual level. She needs you to lead her now more than ever. She needs to see the grace and mercy and love that typifies Christ. She needs to be helped through this process, and God has seen fit to give you to her to help her with that.

Part of praying for her spiritually may be that you need to examine yourself spiritually as well. Do not be afraid to "go on a journey" to be able to become the man, the husband, and the leader you need to be to lead your wife—and even your family—spiritually.

Read the Bible with Her.

So, let's take this whole spiritual discussion a step further and say this: you need to read the Bible with her. Maybe you don't typically do that. Well...now is a good time to start. Maybe you say you don't know where to read from the Bible. Well, that is a legitimate statement. So, here are some suggestions of verses or passages to read. Most of these passages are found in the book of Psalms, which is a tremendous resource:

Psalm 1	Psalm 4	Psalm 16
Psalm 23	Psalm 77	Matthew 5:3-11
Psalm 103	Psalm 4	Psalm 119:73-80
Psalm 139	Psalm 30	Psalm 119:89-96
Psalm 40	Psalm 121	2 Cor. 12:1-10

There is great comfort that comes from reading and meditating on God's word. As Psalm 1 reminds us, there is a blessing that comes from reading and meditating on God's word. So, be faithful to read the Bible and meditate on the word of God with your wife. This will not only help her, but it will certainly help you as a husband, father, and leader. Take the time to read and meditate on the passages above and allow the word of God to refresh your soul and the soul of your wife. God's word will not return void.

Be Prepared for the Fourth Trimester.

To you who are math geniuses, I do want to acknowledge up front that I am fully aware of the mathematical fallacy that is "fourth trimester." I readily concede that this is an oxymoron. However, I am asking you to concede that not everything in life fits nicely into mathematical equations and formulas. There actually is a phenomenon known as "the fourth trimester." It is, in essence, all of the things that are "triggers" beyond the actual nine months of gestation for the pregnancy.

There are several ways that this will play out. Your wife is in the grocery store, and it is three months after the due date of the baby you lost, and she pushes her cart through the cereal aisle only to notice another lady with her baby in a car seat. She smiles as she passes the lady and her baby, and she politely says, "How cute! How old is he?" The lady thanks her for noticing her baby and then replies, "He is three months old." At that moment, your wife begins to tear up and quickly leaves the aisle. Not sure what happened or why it happened, the other lady is left speechless. If you are there with her, you will probably be just as speechless.

Another scenario is that it is September 24. It is a normal, average day. Summer is over, and fall is quickly approaching. You notice that your wife is behaving a bit different today, but you can't put your finger on why. You assume it is because you forgot to do something or because you said something insensitively once again to her. However, as you think back, you realize that, for once, you haven't botched things up. That is when you get the courage to venture in for the conversation, "Honey, are you doing okay? You seem to be frustrated or upset about something." What happens next shocks you. She responds by breaking out in tears and burying her face in your shoulder and telling you as she sobs, "Our baby would have been one year old today." In that moment, I would highly recommend that you wrap your arms around her and hold her. You may ask for how long, and the answer would be, for as long as you need to!

Both of these and countless other scenarios are what is known as "the fourth trimester." It is when something occurs that will trigger an emotional response in your wife. These triggers can come at any moment, in any situation, and they are not limited to the first three to six months after the miscarriage. I know that most of you may be able to relate and, right now, you may be having that "aha moment" where you finally figured out what happened last week or a few months ago.

So how should you respond? Well, for one, be aware that this is a possibility. Do not minimize the situation or her feelings. Saying things like, "Are you serious?" "That triggered you?" "You can't still be dealing with this stuff!?" or "When is this going to stop?" will not help the situation or your relationship. Yes, she is still dealing with the effects of the miscarriage, and your job is not to question it. Your job is to graciously love her. Follow the steps we outlined above and continue to repeat them until she can be in a place where she can completely deal with the miscarriage.

It may be possible that, if things continue to be triggers for her, you need to get some help for her by seeing a counselor. There are so many things that could be going on with her that she needs to get help to talk through and work through these matters. If that is something she needs, then do your best to get her the help she needs. Do not be embarrassed or feel like a failure. Instead, this is one of the best ways to show love to her through these situations. Seek out a pastor or, if need be, seek out a biblical counselor who will be able to help her and help you as well.

Girls, What Can You Do for Him?

Okay, so this book is geared to men. That's why the title is what it is! However, I know that there will be some women, hopefully more than some, who will be interested in helping their husbands work through the miscarriage. So, here is a little section for them to consider. These are some ways that the woman can help and engage with the man during a miscarriage. We will keep this simple because, well, guys aren't too complicated and, as we have mentioned, not many people talk about this stuff—let alone with guys.

Ask Him.

I know the natural question to this is, "Ask him *what?*" So, here goes. Ask him anything. Most guys won't just come out and talk about their feelings. In the case of a miscarriage, most guys don't even know what they are feeling or what they are going through emotionally. So, women, ask him anything. Ask him what he is thinking about when it comes to the miscarriage. Ask him if he is feeling anything. If so, what is it? Ask him if he is scared, nervous, sad, mad, or discouraged. Whatever you can think of to ask, then ask him. No question is off limits. Guys, no question your wife asks can be off limits. You don't necessarily know what you are feeling, and neither does she, so let her ask anything to try to help you as best she can. Women, he may be tempted to be difficult because, well, we're talking about feelings. Be gracious but be persistent. Guys, don't be difficult for your wives during this time!

Assure Him.

I mentioned in chapter one entitled, "It's just a miscarriage," that I felt like my manhood had been called into question with the miscarriage. Ladies, you probably won't understand that and, to be completely honest, I don't know if I could clearly explain it. For a man, having a baby is evidence of his manhood. It is just as simple as that. We don't necessarily want to have a ton of children, but we generally want to have at least one. One child proves we've "got what it takes." It may sound weird or crass to you as women, but to us as guys it makes total sense. So, here is the deal. When we go through a miscarriage, it is like taking a big swing at the ball and missing entirely. We may feel ashamed, we may feel like we are incapable, or we may feel like we aren't real men. So, one of the things that you can do for your man during this time is to assure him.

Assure him that you love him. Assure him that miscarriage isn't somehow his fault or a knock in some way on his manhood. Assure him that you are okay physically or at least that you will be okay physically. Speaking of the aspect of being okay physically, ladies, the whole miscarriage thing is really strange to us as guys. Remember, we are happy it is you that is having the baby and not us. However, if you start talking about hemorrhaging blood and clots and tissue and stuff coming out of you, that creeps a lot of us out. So, it is okay to talk about that, and we know somewhere deep down you need to talk about that but, along with that discussion, you need to assure us that you are okay. Guys envision a scene out of a horror movie when you start talking about some of the things that are happening to you. Get into the details, if necessary, but remember to remind your husband that you are physically okay now or, at least, that you will be okay.

Be Patient with Him.

Women, I cannot stress this next point enough. Do not *force*, *nag*, *guilt*, or *manipulate* your man into talking. You need to be patient with him. This is why, if you can ask him open-ended questions, you will help him to begin to have a dialog with you. But under no circumstance should you push him beyond the extent to which he is willing to talk. He may not say anything. He may say he doesn't want to talk. He may say he isn't affected. If you sit him down like a child and tell him to talk to you, this will drive a wedge between you. A note to the guys here. Dude, don't be a stubborn hold-out on your wife. Keep the communication lines open with her.

Women, there is very little, if anything, written on the topic of how a miscarriage affects a man. Therefore, you are going to need to be discerning, sensitive, and flexible when it comes to him discussing things with you. Don't compare him with other men. Don't talk about how your friend's husband shared this or that. Don't take it personally if he isn't ready to talk about it. Be patient with him. Be caring and sensitive to him and let him deal with things as God deals with him. As a side note, it may be a year or two or more before he is able to articulate things to the point of talking about them. Personally, I can talk about things much better now, more than a decade removed from our fourth miscarriage, than I could then. So, ladies, please, please be patient. This is new territory for everyone!

Encourage Him.

Ladies, encourage your husband to spend time with friends. Even if it is just a group of guys hanging out. He needs to have that outlet as well. Yes, he needs to take care of you, and he needs to make sure that you are good, but he also needs to just be a guy. He needs to be able to hang out, eat wings, watch a game, go golfing, or whatever it is he finds as an enjoyable form of relaxation. It is through these times that he will be more likely to open up. Again, society says that guys don't struggle in any way shape or form with a miscarriage. So, be patient with him, but also encourage him to be a guy and to talk to his friends. This will help him to be more likely to open up to you.

A note to guys: you cannot take advantage of your wife or exploit this particular aspect of dealing with miscarriage by continually trying to get her to "let you go out." You need to be sure to be there for her, to love her, to pray with her, and to do all the things we talked about. If you aren't doing those things, you shouldn't be pushing to go out with your friends. Be sensitive to this situation and to your wife.

Pray for Him.

Ladies, one of the greatest things you can do for your husband is to pray for him. Pray that he would have the strength and grace he needs as he helps you and ministers to you and to your children. Pray that he would stay faithful to God and His Word. Pray that he would be encouraged as he goes about his daily routine. Pray that he would not become embittered against God or against you in some way. Pray for him. Pray that God will work in his life as He seems fit. Pray that he would grow spiritually and that he would be honest about getting the help he needs.

A Take Away...

This is to both men and women, to both husband and wife. God loves you both. God cares for you both. God is sufficient for you both. However, there are very few situations in a marriage that could potentially drive a wedge between the two of you like a miscarriage because of all of the consequences this has for your family and your future. You need God, but you need one another as well. Take the time you both need to be sure you are there for each other. Guys, another guy cannot do this for your wife. Women, another woman cannot do this for your husband. God has given you both to each other and, if you recall in your vows, you probably said something to the effect that you would be there for each other when life is great and when life stinks. Well, in this case, the elephant is in the room, and he is making a mess all over the place, and it stinks. So, trust in God, rely on His strength, plug your nose, and dive into your relationship with one another.

CHAPTER 4

"NO CATCHER?": HELPING YOUR CHILDREN THROUGH MISCARRIAGE

So here is the order of "concern" when it comes to how people respond to miscarriages: first is the wife, second is the husband, and third are the kids. As we have established, the husband is often forgotten in this process of dealing with a miscarriage. Well, if the husband is often forgotten, the children are not even thought about. If we think that the husband does not have a connection to the pregnancy, then it stands to reason that the children do not have a connection...or so we are tempted to think.

Our Fourth Time....

At the end of December 2005, we excitedly announced to our friends and to our church that Kimberly was expecting not just one baby, but two! Now, having been through the pregnancy and birth of our first son, Caleb, in July

2003, having twins seemed overwhelming, but yet it seemed, weirdly enough, doable. I was still in the same surreal state I was in when I first found out Kimberly was pregnant, but this time it was due to the fact that we were going to have twins!

Something that is important to know about Caleb, our son who was two and a half at this point, is that he absolutely loved baseball (and still does). In fact, when he was nine months old, he could sit in his playpen and literally throw balls across the room. It really was amazing, and I am not just saying that because he is my kid. When we found out we were pregnant and when we knew it was twins, we told Caleb that we were having two babies. Caleb quickly figured out that he would now have, for all practical purposes, a baseball team. He had it all figured out, He was the batter, one of the babies would be the pitcher, and one of them would be the catcher. For Caleb, life was coming together well.

Our lives were a bit crazy the first part of 2006 as we were in the process of transitioning from being youth leaders of a growing, vibrant youth group to beginning to raise support to move to Italy as missionaries. Yet, in the midst of the crazy schedule, Kimberly was progressing well with the twins. We went for a check-up in early March, and we listened to both heartbeats. I can still remember being fascinated that, as the doctor put the listening device in Kimberly's upper rib cage on her left side, we could hear one heartbeat at one rate and then, when she put the listening device down by Kimberly's lower abdomen on her right side, you could hear another heartbeat at a different pace.

Because Kimberly was considered to have a high-risk pregnancy, we had regular check-ups. Towards the end of

March, we went back for a check-up. The doctor again began to listen for the heartbeats and, this time, it was harder to differentiate if there were two different heart rates or if they were beating at the same rate or even if there were still two heartbeats. Kimberly, at this point, was five-and-a half months along in her pregnancy. The doctor wanted to be sure about what was happening and, so, she had us schedule an appointment with an ultrasound specialist. So, we setup an appointment for two weeks later with a specialist at a different location.

If we were to be honest, we probably suspected something wasn't right when we were in the doctor's office listening for heartbeats (We had been down this road before.). The doctor wasn't overly alarmed, but she was alarmed enough to think that something may not be right. We absolutely loved our OB/GYN. She was kind, compassionate, and willing to listen to us. She epitomized what you would think a doctor should be. Contrasting that was the ultrasound specialist we went to see.

We arrived for the appointment with the specialist on a beautiful, sunny, end-of-March day in Farmington, New Mexico. We had Caleb with us, as we didn't have anyone to really watch him and didn't really think it would be a problem having him there. Honestly, I didn't even think he was all that aware of what was going on. We went into the room, and the tech immediately began doing the ultrasound. He ran the probe over Kimberly's stomach a couple of times and then said, with an irritated tone, "They actually told you there were two babies in there?" Kind of shocked and taken back, I replied, "Yes, we have had regular check-ups, and we have heard both heartbeats." He, with all the tact that could apparently be uttered by someone who hated his job, said, "I don't know why they told you that. You don't have twins; you only have one baby." He pulled the probe off Kimberly, wiped off the gel, closed down his ultrasound machine, and walked out of the room.

To say that we were shocked with how the news was broken to us would be an understatement. The non-existent tact of the tech was absolutely horrendous. And while we were left in shock and trying to process everything that the tech had just told us, he quickly closed up his machine, said goodbye, and left the room. There we were, all three of us just standing there and Kimberly and I thinking it was just the two of us trying to process the news. Then, that is when our reality came crashing down. From across the room came a soft-spoken voice in a confused and questioning tone that said, "No Catcher?"

What had been a perceived issue between Kimberly and me suddenly became an issue for our entire family. What we never realized until that very moment was that our child, although only two and a half, had been acutely impacted by the news that we had lost the other baby. I had no idea that children that young could even be aware of things going on around them like this. We should have known better. Caleb knew Kimberly was going to have a baby. He could see her belly getting bigger, but we totally missed the concept that he was actually tracking along. So, let's talk about how to deal with your children as you go through a miscarriage.

Just to clear things up, what had actually happened to Kimberly was actually something called vanishing twin syndrome. Fortunately for Kimberly, she had just read about that a few weeks earlier. She had not informed me of her new-found information, so the whole concept took a bit for me to process. Vanishing twin syndrome is where the baby that dies is absorbed by the body. Don't ask me how that all works; even now, years later, it is a bit creepy to think about. If you knew Andrew, our twin that made it, you would understand this in some way as he has enough personality for two people. We often joke that he absorbed the other twin's personality!

So, back to the kids...

Okay, so if you have no children when you go through a miscarriage, then you may think that this section may not be for you right now. I want to assure you that that is what I thought as well. However, if you would like to know how to help your kids through this, whether born or unborn at the moment, or if you want to help others through this, then this section will hopefully be helpful for you.

Helping Your Born Children...

Whether you realize it or not, your children are actually affected by a miscarriage as well. Now, the mother may not have been far enough along that she was telling people that she was pregnant. If that is the case, the effects will be minimized to some degree with your children. However, if you are like us and actually have your two-and-a-half-year-old in the room with you when you find out that your expected child has died, then that is something you most definitely will have to deal with. So, what are some things you can do to help your kids through this time?

1. *Be honest with them.* Men, your kids can handle more
   than you realize sometimes. Do not lie to your kids.
   Be honest with them. Tell them the truth. Tell them
   that the baby has died. Tell them that their mommy is
   going to be okay. Tell them that God is in control and
   that He loves them. Tell them Scripture passages you
   both can read to be reassured, encouraged, and
   strengthened. Do it with tact, with grace, and with
   love, but tell them the truth. Some parents are
   tempted, in an attempt to help their children, to
   actually be deceptive with them. This may seem like a
   good thing at the time but, in time, this will be a
   problem for you as a parent.

   I know that it is not always easy to be honest with the
   kids. You don't know what to say, and you don't
   know what they will understand. You also don't want
   to overwhelm them with the news. So, be sensitive to
   the right time and place to share with them and, also,
   be sensitive as to what they are ready to hear. But rest
   assured, your children will be able to navigate a
   miscarriage with your help. It may surprise you that,
   in the initial conversations your children will actually
   not talk about the miscarriage a whole lot, but rather
   will just take the situation all in.

2. *Let them talk about it.* I have been amazed at when and
   where my children decide they want to talk about our
   miscarriages. However, one of the things we have
   never done is told them that they cannot talk about it.
   I have found that the conversations usually don't last
   a long time. Maybe a minute or two at random times
   every so often. Whenever your kids decide they want

to talk about miscarriage, let them talk about it. Don't tell them to be quiet. Don't tell them it doesn't affect them. Don't discourage them in any way from having a healthy conversation about it. Maybe the time when they bring the topic up is not necessarily an appropriate time. If that is the case, then let them know you will discuss it later. However, you must actually discuss it later with them.

Just like you and your wife, your children need to process through the realities of life, including the realities of a miscarriage. This may make you uncomfortable, but this is healthy for your children. It is okay to not have all of the answers for them, but you need to let them process as much as you can. Your pastor can help you with this as well. In fact, it may be helpful to have your kids talk to someone else while you are in the room with them. This will help you, and it will help them.

3. *Let them cry if they need to.* I am not a fan of crying. Remember, it is the whole "warm and fuzzy" thing. However, when it comes to your kids and, quite honestly, to your wife as well, do not be afraid to let them cry. Caleb was devastated when he found out his masterful plan for a three–person baseball team was no longer going to occur. It's okay. Let them cry. Let them deal with it. Shoot—If you need to cry, then cry. Handle this situation with love, understanding, and compassion. Be gracious and be understanding. Your children will respond differently than you and, quite honestly, differently than each other. Handle each child in his or her own unique way.

4. *Encourage them with the Bible.* Your kids are going to have questions. Maybe even some questions you don't know how to answer. That's okay. Take them to the Bible to encourage them and to help them through this. If you don't know the Bible that well, that is okay. Find someone who can help you with that. Your pastor would be more than happy to help you with that. If he isn't able or willing to help you, then you probably need a new pastor or new church. If you don't go to church, then ask around for a church that has a pastor who could help you. Find a friend who is a committed believer and ask him for help. God has provided you the resources you need in His Word.

5. *Help them with tact.* Kids are great. They say the most embarrassing things—and mostly at the wrong times, don't they? When it comes to the matter of a miscarriage, your children may say some things that will make you cringe. It's okay! While you are working through a miscarriage experience with with them, give them some examples of what would be appropriate to say and maybe some examples of what would not be appropriate to say. This is a chance for you to give maturing guidance to your children. If you need to laugh, then laugh. Some of the things they may say may be funny. Pray that God will give you the wisdom you need in order to help them process things appropriately.

Helping Your Unborn Children...

One of the ways we did not expect to have to deal with a miscarriage was with Andrew our son, who was the twin, and our daughter Rebecca, who was born two years after Andrew. In my mind, a miscarriage happens, you deal with it, and you move on. The unborn kids are none the wiser, and you just help the children you have that are already born, and life is beautiful right? Wrong! Let me introduce you to Abby Deets.

My wife and I have three living children: Caleb, Andrew, and Rebecca. We have four children who are in Heaven. We did not name any of the kids we lost to miscarriage; we did not really do anything for them. That was our decision. I know that some families will handle this differently, and that is perfectly fine. However, for us, we thought we had dealt with things once we got Caleb beyond the fact that there would be no catcher. Fast forward about three years, and I will explain.

It was a Sunday morning, and we were getting ready for church. The boys were in their room talking about who knows what. Caleb would have been about six, and Andrew would have been about three. All of a sudden, from out of their room, we heard Andrew in a loud, questioning voice say, "I had a twin?!" There is something inside you that reminds you, "Oh man, maybe we should have had this conversation." I guess it is a lot like parents who wait to inform their children that they are adopted. Only to realize, to their horror, that someone else beat them to the conversation.

I was not ready for the conversation, and I am not sure Kimberly was either, but, like the trooper she is, she handled this in stride. Here is what has happened with us and Andrew in the time since he discovered that he was a twin and that we had lost his twin before birth:

1. *He has come up with the gender of the twin.* I am not exactly sure what the thinking was in Andrew's mind, but he has determined, much to the dismay of Caleb who had pre-planned the baseball team, that the twin that died was a girl. (Not that we are saying girls can't play baseball. I grew up in the home of the Rockford Peaches, after all.) We never knew the gender of the baby, so Andrew's guess is as good as ours. Hey, we both have a 50/50 chance of being right! For him, he felt that he was certain that the baby that died was a girl. So, Andrew had determined the gender of our baby. It's okay that he believes that his twin was a girl.

2. *He has come up with the name of the twin: Abby Deets.* This is the name that Andrew has given to his twin. It helps him to have a name to put with the miscarriage. For him, it has a more tangible feel to it that it isn't just "the twin" or "the baby." To him, it is his sister, Abby Deets. It may seem strange to you that he felt a need to name his twin. This was a challenge for me as well but, for Andrew, this was a meaningful act. Allowing Andrew to put a name to the loss of life experienced through miscarriage has been one of the most meaningful things he has done. Even now, he has a dog named Abby. It has real significance to Andrew, and that is okay.

3. *He has come up with a means of remembering the twin.* When Andrew was seven, we moved to Grand Rapids, Michigan. In the church that I pastored, we had a family that was involved in a significant ministry of helping ladies who had had abortions. As a means of helping women deal with this, these family members

started the Garden of Hope, where women could have the names of the babies etched in a stone monument and permanently remembered. This was and is very therapeutic for these women as they sought help after their abortions. Andrew has always been fascinated by this ministry. He loves the idea of a permanent place to remember the babies that have died. Through the course of time, he got the courage to talk to the lady who is in charge of the memorial. She was so gracious to allow him to not only express his heart's desire, but also to follow through on that desire to remember Abby. Today, there is a name written on that stone monument in Grand Rapids with the name Abby Deets, and that is okay.

4. *He speaks often of the twin.* To know Andrew is to almost certainly know that he had a twin. Andrew speaks often of the baby we lost. In fact, he speaks of it more often than we do. To him, this is part of his identity. As I mentioned, he has named his dog Abby and, if he were allowed, would probably have a tattoo with her name. I think the whole idea of talking about her and remembering his twin has much more significance to him than it does even to us at times. His brother has a hard time understanding why Andrew needs to talk about Abby like that, but he does. For Andrew, this is part of the grieving process, and that is okay.

So, how should you help your children who were not born when the miscarriage happened?

1. *Let them remember.*
2. *Let them ask about it.*
3. *Let them process as they need.*

A Take Away…

I fully understand that each child and each situation is going to be unique. For us, Andrew has handled this in a different way than we probably ever would have imagined. Here is the biggest piece of advice that I can offer to you. Let your child deal with this in whatever appropriate way he or she wants to. Do not downplay this or act like it isn't a real need that they have. It would be tempting to do that, but you will only cause major problems down the road for the child and for you and your relationship. Again, each situation will be different, but you need to be gracious and sensitive enough to allow your child to grieve in his or her own way. This is what this is—this is a death, and there is a grieving process that needs to occur. Do not be so insensitive that you do not allow your kids or your wife or you for that matter to grieve in an appropriate manner.

Indulge Me for Another Minute…

I would have been perfectly happy ignoring the fact that we had four miscarriages. I would have been perfectly content to chalk that up to the "problems of life" and to never have talked about our miscarriages, or anyone else's for that matter. I would have been even happier not writing a book about miscarriage. The biggest reason this book exists is because I had to deal with Andrew. I would have let it go and never discussed it had it not been for his persistence over his lifetime to deal with it. I cannot express how thankful I am that Andrew never gave up dealing with this because, by default, I have been able to deal with it. You never know what God will bring into your life to get you to address things. I, for one, am thankful that Andrew never gave up on dealing with his loss. I am thankful that God has helped me to deal with the miscarriages we had. My regret is that I did not do this sooner and on my own accord.

CHAPTER 5

FINDING HOPE EVEN WHEN YOU DIDN'T KNOW IT WAS MISSING

So, we mentioned at the beginning that this book is unapologetically written from a Biblical perspective. By that I mean that everything that is taught and written in this book is written from the standpoint that Jesus Christ is the One who died on the cross to save us from our sins, that our sufficiency is found in Christ alone, and that God's Word, the Bible, has the answers for all of the challenges we face in life.

We have spent the vast majority of this book dealing with the various aspects of a miscarriage from a man's standpoint. This chapter will exclusively deal with finding hope in the midst of the miscarriage. You may not have any idea that you have lost hope or that you even need hope, but it is very possible that, whatever stage of life you are at spiritually, this chapter will have encouragement for you. This chapter is intended to help you think through the various experiences you have had with your miscarriage and to deal with them in as Biblical a manner as possible. For some, this will be totally foreign. That is okay. Take your time and process through the following section. For others, this will be a good review and, hopefully, an encouragement as you are reminded of the hope we have in Jesus Christ.

In the Bible, there is a letter that was written to a group of Christians in the city of Colossae. Colossae was an ancient city on the west side of modern-day Turkey. Paul wrote this letter to the church when he was in prison in Rome. This is the book of Colossians. His purpose in writing the letter was to help us to focus on matters of Heaven as opposed to focusing on earthly things. In fact, in one of the sections we focus on below (2:8-13), Paul reminds us that self-abuse, beating ourselves up physically or emotionally, is not the answer to anything. This letter shows Christ for who He really is: the preeminent God.

So, I encourage you to grab a Bible, or pull it up on your phone, and let's briefly work our way through these verses. We will keep this simple and short so that you can work your way through this without too much issue. The numbers in the parenthesis refer to the chapter and verses in Colossians that we will examine in each section.

Life Is Found in Christ Alone (1:15-17).

Here is the simple truth of this section: Jesus Christ is in charge of everything. He made everything, He owns everything, and He holds everything together. Nothing happens that He does not allow. So, when you and your wife are tempted to think that somehow you had something to do with the miscarriage or that you should have done something differently in order to avoid having the miscarriage, just know this: Jesus Christ is the One who literally holds all of this universe together. Jesus Christ is in charge of all life. No one is born and no one dies without decree of Jesus Christ.

This does not mean that we blame God for the miscarriage. God has obviously allowed the miscarriage to happen. There are consequences of Adam and Eve's sin that are impacting this world. One of those consequences is miscarriage. However, Christ *has* allowed this to happen, and Christ has specifically allowed this to happen to you. He has a plan and a purpose for what He is doing. You do not need to blame yourself or your wife. You don't need to blame God either. You can trust Him that He is working out His will in your life and that He is completely in control of the situation. This was His baby, this was His creation that He gave to you, and, in His wisdom and providence, He has taken His baby away. Like Job, we are not to blame God. We simply say, "The Lord gives, and the Lord takes away; blessed be the name of the Lord."

I know that for some who are reading this, this idea may sound trite or callous. That is certainly understandable. However, when you realize that Christ is the One who holds all things together, you have to then conclude that He is the giver and taker of life. It was God who brought this baby into existence through conception, and it was God who began to form the inward parts of the baby. For whatever reason, God has seen fit to allow this baby to no longer grow and develop and come to term. God is the author of life. He is the giver and taker of life and, though we may not understand all of that, we praise His name for what He allows to happen.

Your Hope Is Found in Christ Alone (1:18-23).

Paul makes perfectly clear in these verses that Jesus Christ came to earth to reconcile you to God. What does the word *reconcile* mean? It means to set up a relationship of peace that did not exist before. You see, the Bible tells us that we were enemies of God. Paul here in Colossians says we were alienated from God and hostile in mind toward Him in doing evil deeds. Because we were enemies of God, we behaved in a way that was offensive to Him and His nature. God is holy and, clearly, Paul makes note that we are not.

So, how does a holy God and an evil, wicked person have a peaceful relationship? It is only through the death and resurrection of Jesus Christ. Paul says that it was through the death of Jesus Christ that we could be reconciled to God. You see, because of man's sin, the consequence for us and all mankind, for that matter, is death (See Romans 3:23 and 5:12). That death was both literal and representative. We literally die because of our sin. But that death also represents where we go when we die. We will spend eternity in Hell because of our sin (See Luke 12:5 and Revelation 21:8).

You may say, "That is not a good thing to read about." You are correct! That is not good news for anyone. But wherever there is bad news, it means that there is hope for good news. Here is the good news. The Bible tells us that God loved us so much (amazing, isn't it?) that He sent Jesus Christ, His Son, to die for us (See John 3:16 and Romans 5:8). Through the death of Jesus Christ, as Paul mentions here, He paid for the sins of mankind (See I John 2:2).

So, what do you need to do in order to receive this reconciliation that Paul talks about? Well, it is this: you need to submit to Jesus Christ as Lord and trust Him to be your Savior (See Romans 10:9-13). Jesus Christ came and took your place. It should have been you who died for your sins, but Jesus Christ took our sins on Himself and paid the penalty of death for us. He then rose from the dead to show He had power and victory over death (See I Corinthians 15). That is the good news—the gospel. This is the only hope any of us have. Without the gospel, there is no hope for any of us.

As you go through this process of miscarriage, if you do not know Jesus Christ as Savior, there is not a lot of hope that can be given to you. In essence, you are on your own just trying to figure it out. This is why people turn to various other things to find "hope". If, however, you do know Jesus Christ as your Savior, you have the peace and the hope that is beyond comprehension (See Philippians 4:7).

You Can Rejoice in Christ Alone (1:24-2:5).

Paul now talks about rejoicing in his sufferings. Paul was talking about the persecution he faced and the suffering he went through for the cause of Christ. We aren't trying to say that having a miscarriage is the same as being persecuted for Christ, but here is something we can pull out of this. It is possible to rejoice, even in the midst of trials and tragedies. But here is the important thing: we rejoice not in the event itself, but we rejoice because of Jesus Christ. Let me explain.

Having a miscarriage is a tragedy in and of itself. A life has been taken and will never have an opportunity to live on this earth. But this isn't just "a baby"; it is *God's child that was given to you*. Your baby girl or boy will never experience the life you have experienced. That is a tragedy, and that tragedy creates a trial in your life. How will you respond? How will you deal with this? Will you be bitter? Will you go into denial? Will you blame someone? Will you be angry? Will you rejoice? That's right, will you rejoice?

For some of you, I just offended you. Right now, you are thinking I must be out of my mind to have asked, "Will you rejoice?" But let me just stop you right there. Paul is writing about suffering, and he is talking about rejoicing in the suffering that is being endured. He isn't saying he is rejoicing because of the physical events, per se, but rather, he is rejoicing at what the events mean and what the events are accomplishing in his life. Here is the deal: through God and through His sufficient work in your life and in your marriage and through this miscarriage, you can rejoice in Christ. You can rejoice at what He can and will accomplish in your life. You can rejoice that He is sustaining you, and you can rejoice because He is in control of all things.

You Can Be Encouraged in Christ Alone (Confident Faith, 2:6-7).

Paul speaks about our faith that is rooted and built up in Christ. If you have trusted Christ as your Savior, you are a child of God. You have eternal life, and you have a relationship with Jesus Christ. However, your faith—or should we say your relationship with Christ—may be weak. Paul speaks about how we can have a strong and confident faith in, or relationship with, Jesus Christ.

Paul says that, as you have received Christ, [in the same manner] walk in Him. Well, how did we receive Christ? The Bible tells us in Ephesians 2:8-9 that by grace we were saved through faith. We are saved through faith. So, Paul is pointing out that just as we were saved by faith, we walk by faith in Christ. It is this faith, this walk with God, that Paul says is to be rooted and grounded in Christ. In other words, we are to be strong, secure, and unmovable in our faith in Christ. How do we become a seasoned "faith walker"? We do it by going through the difficult times in life and trusting God in the process. We become rooted and grounded by trusting God to work in our lives in the midst of tragedies. We become rooted and grounded in our faith by knowing God for who He is, trusting Him as He works in our lives, and by clinging to Him in the midst of the storms.

As we mentioned earlier, there will be those who will discourage you in this process of having a miscarriage, but you have access to the One who is the all-sufficient source of strength and encouragement. His name is Jesus Christ, and He wants to comfort you, sustain you, encourage you, and help you through this time. Will you allow Him to do that?

Your Identity Is in Christ Alone (2:8-23).

It was common in the day Paul was writing this section of Colossians for people to do all sorts of self-abusive actions on themselves. They would do anything they could to try to prove their religious loyalty or their loyalty to a particular person. For them, their identities, or who they were, were found in their actions. As many people as there were who were willing to engage in these self-abusive actions, there were also plenty of people that were willing to guilt them into doing them. The societal pressure was tremendous. This is why Paul addresses the matter of not allowing the philosophy of men to take you captive.

Our society today is no different. There are a number of things with which society will try to take you captive with in terms of philosophy. The same thing Paul said to the believers at Colossae is the same thing he would say to us today: your identity or self-worth is not found in what the world deems important. Your identity and self-worth are found in Jesus Christ. In other words, do not allow yourselves to buy the lie that says if you do not have kids, you are worthless. Do not allow yourselves to buy the lie that says if you don't have a big house and brand-new cars, you are worthless. Do not allow yourselves to buy the lie that says if your kids do not excel at sports, you are worthless.

The world's philosophy will try to consume you to the point where you become enslaved to the things of this world in order to gain the approval of society. Instead, you need to understand that your identity, who you are, is found in what Christ sees you as. Paul has already mentioned in Colossians that you have been redeemed and reconciled and transferred from the kingdom of darkness to the kingdom of light. If you know Christ as your Savior, then this is who you are in Christ.

There will be plenty of people who will try to convince you that your worth or identity is found in status, in material possessions, in popularity, in whatever. Christ, however, tells you that you are loved, valued, and held in high esteem by Him no matter what. Embrace the fact that your identity is found in Christ and not in the world's philosophy. Regardless of how many miscarriages you have or regardless of whether or not you ever have children, your identity can and must be in Christ.

Your Focus Must Be on Christ Alone (3:1-17).

Peace is an elusive thing. We hope for it, search for it, and long for it. However, Paul says that we are to let the peace of Christ rule—or have authority—in our lives. The peace of Christ is supposed to be in charge in our lives as we handle the various trials and tragedies that life presents to us. How do we do that? How do we let the peace of Christ rule and reign in our lives? Paul says it happens when we focus on Christ and Christ alone.

When you go through a situation like a miscarriage, you will be tempted to focus on a lot of different things: the stupid things people say to you, the health of your wife, the frustration of not being in control, the difficulty you now must deal with emotionally. There are plenty of things that will rob your focus and attention—the very things that robbed me of my focus and attention. Paul says here that we are to focus on Christ; we are to focus on things that are above. We are to focus on heavenly things. We are to focus on who Christ is, what Christ has done, and what Christ is doing and wants to do in our lives.

You have gone through, or are going through, a traumatic experience. Where is your focus? Is it on yourself and your circumstances? Is it on your wife and her struggles, or is it on Christ? Are you focused on the fact that He holds all things together? Are you focused on the work He is doing in your life to help you be more rooted and grounded in your faith? Are you focused on His love, care, and grace for you? What are you focused on at this time?

A Take Away...

If you have never trusted Christ as your Savior, then there is no better time than right now. You can do this at any time, but right now works really well. It begins by realizing that you have a broken relationship with Christ because of sin. You realize that Jesus Christ paid the penalty of your sin, which was death and eternal separation from Him in Hell and that, without His sacrifice, you would have no hope. You realize that you cannot save yourself by your good works or anything else you could do on your own. You turn to Christ in submission to who He is and what He has done and trust Him as your Savior. There is no greater thing you could do than that.

If you have trusted Christ as Savior, then I would encourage you to engage in a solid, Bible-preaching church where you can grow in God's Word through the regular teaching of the Bible and through small group relationships with other believers who will help to encourage you as you become rooted and grounded in your faith in Jesus Christ. If you are already a believer, how is your hope or confidence amidst this situation?

As you navigate the difficult waters of a miscarriage both now and into the future, you will be confronted with many things. Namely, you will be confronted with your insufficiency. You are insufficient to bring your pregnancy to full term with a healthy baby. You are insufficient to keep your wife from having a miscarriage. You are insufficient to deal with the emotional, physical, or spiritual struggles that come as a result of the miscarriage. You are insufficient to always deal graciously with the hurtful things people say. You are insufficient to be okay by simply hiding your feelings as a man deeply inside of you. The point is, as brutally honest as we can be, you are insufficient.

However, what Paul presents in Colossians is that we have someone who is all-sufficient. That person, Jesus Christ, stands ready to be everything we cannot be. So, we can respond by trusting ourselves, insufficient as we may be, or trusting in the all-sufficiency of Jesus Christ. He wants you to come to Him just as you are. Come with your brokenness, come with your hurt, come with your "wounds", come with whatever you have left. But do this one thing: come to Christ. He alone will sustain you and your wife and your family.

THE END

Well, as we all know, this isn't really the end. In fact, it may be just the beginning! We have taken you through a lot of different thoughts, ideas, and questions to consider in this project. I can say, as someone who has been where you are, that this is not necessarily an easy road to be going down. But I want to assure you that it is a road that can lead to a fulfilled relationship in Jesus Christ if you allow God to work as He wants to.

Remember, you can't and shouldn't do this on your own. You need help, you need encouragement, you need support. Make sure you get the help you need, and make sure your wife gets the help she needs. You are not Superman, and neither is your wife. I encourage you both to get the help and encouragement you both need.

Find a church, if you don't already have one, that will help you grow in your relationship with Christ—a church that will help you with building friendships and relationships that will help you as you continue to grow in Christ. Find those who may have gone through what you have been through and ask them for help as you go through this time in your life.

Go have fun! Sometimes it is easy to get so bogged down in the physical, emotional, and even spiritual side of a miscarriage that we forget to have fun. Go find your friends and hang out. Be crazy, be goofy, and just have fun. Sometimes that is therapeutic in and of itself as you allow yourselves to forget about some of the things that you have been going through.

Help others. You have been given a gift. It is the gift of knowing what it is like to have gone through a miscarriage. The unfortunate thing is that it is very likely you will soon become "the expert" as you become "that couple" that had the miscarriage. Within three months of our first miscarriage, Kimberly and I were introduced to and helped a number of people who had had miscarriages. Trust me, it will happen to you, and you are in a good place to be able to provide them help, even if it is as simple as giving them this book or something similar.

I hope that as you have read this book, you have not encountered anything offensive in what was written as far as how to deal with the miscarriage. My intent, certainly, was not to be offensive, insensitive, or callous in any way, shape, or form. This is a challenging topic and one that is very sensitive for many people. Please know that the grace of Christ is sufficient to help you through this time. Please know that my prayer for you and your wife is that you would have peace and resolution in this matter. I trust that, in some way, I have been able to help you with that.

The End

Thank you for taking the time to read this. I hope it has been a blessing and an encouragement to you in your journey that God has allowed you to go on. I hope that God will do a work in you like He has done in my own life.

Dave

FREQUENTLY WONDERED-ABOUT QUESTIONS

Many times, a manual or another informational resource will have a frequently-asked-questions section. Well, knowing how little miscarriage is talked about and how little is said about this topic, I can say that these are not questions that are frequently asked. However, these are, no doubt, some of the questions you have had, but instead of asking them, you have simply just wondered about them.

What Should We Say?

Whenever we go through dark waters with our friends or family, it is vitally important that we be real, genuine, and yet sensitive at the same time. So here are a few things (though certainly not exhaustive) that you should focus on as you seek to minister to those who have experienced a miscarriage:

1. *God's faithfulness* (Exodus 34:6, Deuteronomy 31:6, Psalm 33:4, Psalm 91:4, Psalm 119:90, Lamentations 3:22-23, 1 Corinthians 1:9, 1 Corinthians 10:13, 2 Thessalonians 3:3, 2 Timothy 2:13)

2. *God's grace* (John 1:14, Acts 20:24, 2 Corinthians 8:7, 2 Corinthians 12:9, Ephesians 1:7, Ephesians 4:7, Hebrews 4:16)

3. *God's strength* (Joshua 1:9, Psalm 46:1-3, Psalm 73:26, Isaiah 40:29, Isaiah 41:10, I Corinthians 16:13, 2 Corinthians 12:10, Philippians 4:13, I Peter 5:10)

4. *God's love* (Psalm 5:11-12, Psalm 36:5-7, Romans 8:35-39, Ephesians 3:18-19, I John 4:18)

5. *God's peace* (Roman 5:1, Ephesians 2:14, Philippians 4:7, Colossians 3:15, 2 Thessalonians 3:16, Jude 2)

What If We Can't Have Kids?

One of the challenges that a couple is going to have to deal with is the possibility that they cannot have children. Maybe you have had multiple miscarriages and you have finally come to the realization that part of your struggle has to do with an ability to maintain a healthy pregnancy. Dealing with infertility is difficult for a couple to deal with. You need to have many deep and healthy conversations about what your options may be. Some options will be expensive. Some will also be physically and emotionally—and even ethically—difficult to deal with. Consult your physician, consult your pastor, and trust God that He will give you wisdom on how to move forward. There is hope even in infertility. One of the biggest things you could consider is adoption. I know that this can be just as expensive and emotionally difficult of a process as a birth, but what a picture of redemption that can be played out as you adopt an unwanted baby from someone else. If you find yourselves dealing with infertility, then seek to find out how you may be a blessing to an unwanted child. Another option that you may consider is being foster parents. The foster system is overrun with children who need love, care, and support. It may be that God is giving you the opportunity to be a blessing and encouragement to unwanted and abandoned children. At least, would you consider this option?

What If They Won't Talk to Me?

It may be possible that your wife or girlfriend or your husband or boyfriend may be so distraught by the effects of the miscarriage that they simply will not engage you in talking through things. If that is the case, then be patient with them. I would encourage you to do a couple of things:

1. *Love them.* Unconditionally demonstrate your love and affection for them. This will be difficult for you to do for any length of time. However, God intends for you to demonstrate that sacrificial love for them.

2. *Wait for them.* That's it. There's not much else here other than wait.

3. *Encourage them.* One of the things you do need to actively work towards is to get them connected to someone who they can talk to: a pastor, a counselor, a friend—someone who they will be able to open up to and begin to talk through what they are dealing with. You need to be prepared that you may be down the

line a person or two as far as who they open up to. However, if you can encourage them to talk with someone who can help, they will eventually open up to you.

What Are Ways We Can Give Back?

As you go through the process of having a miscarriage, or as you have come out of the time of dealing with the loss in a miscarriage, you may wonder if there is any way for you to be a blessing and encouragement to others. In almost every major city in America, there are pregnancy resource centers. There are literally hundreds of ministries across America dedicated to helping people with pregnancy issues, abortions, other pro-life services for before birth and after birth. It is often therapeutic and encouraging for families who have experienced miscarriage to involve themselves in some form of ministry that is related to pre-birth and post-birth ministry.

Two ministries that I want to specifically mention that have been a blessing to our family are the Omega House and Alpha Grand Rapids, both in Grand Rapids, Michigan. Both ministries have a unique focus of ministry, but they are equally valuable. One of the greatest joys we have had as a family is to involve ourselves personally, and our church corporately, in these ministries. What a joy it has been to be a blessing to encourage these ministries through generous donations and, also, through volunteering our time and energies. This has been a tremendous blessing for us, and I know that it has been an encouragement to these ministries as well. If you live in the Grand Rapids, Michigan area, I would strongly encourage you to find ways to bless these ministries. If you live elsewhere, find similar ministries or ways to be a blessing to those who are in these types of ministries. You will not regret the time and effort put in to bless these ministries.

What about Grandparents?

We have talked about men being left out of the conversation around miscarriage, and we even talked about children being left out of the conversation. However, one thing we did not address is the grandparents. Watching their children go through the agony of miscarriage is difficult on any parent. However, compounded to that is the agony of also knowing you lost a grandbaby. So, in order to help grandparents through this, here are just a few practical steps that you can take:

1. *Let them grieve in their own way.* Don't force or pressure them to grieve in a particular way or in a way that you want. Allow them to process things as naturally as they would like.

2. *Purchase a little memento to allow them to remember the lost baby.* This could be a picture, a knick-knack, a medallion for a necklace, or something else that they can place somewhere special in the house to remember the baby. This will help them process the loss in their own way and in their own time.

3. *Offer whatever encouragement you can through the process.* It is sometimes difficult for children to think about being the ones who are comforting parents. However, in the strange ways life happens, this becomes necessary. Be ready to be there in any way you can to help them through the process. You will deal with things in a

different way than your parents, but that doesn't mean that they won't need help in dealing with the loss of a grandbaby.

4. *Communicate with them on how you are doing.* Parents are always concerned for their children, no matter how old the parents are and no matter how old the children are. This means that your parents want to know how you are doing. So, tell them. Communicate openly about what is going on in your mind, your heart, and your head. This will help them process through things as well.

5. *Ask them how they are doing.* Remember, this is a loss for your parents as well. They were expecting to be grandparents with all the expectations and joys that come with being grandparents. So, make sure you check on them to see how they are doing.

6. *Grieve together.* This is something you each will process through differently and, yet, at the same time, it is something that you can process through together. Never underestimate the bond that can develop when you go through the grieving process together.

How Can I Help Other Guys?

Guys often do not do well engaging one another in deeper, more sensitive conversations. So, this may be a challenge for you or for your guy friend who is going through a miscarriage. However, here are a few suggestions to encourage you to engage him as best as possible:

1. *Offer to just hang out.* Guys aren't always good at talking. You know that, so go with it. Tell your buddy you just want to hang out. Nothing more. No expectations. Just two dudes hanging out playing ball, watching a game, or whatever you enjoy doing. This will help more than you know.

2. *Bring up the topic naturally.* Do not force the issue, but as the conversations move to a point where it is natural to talk about the topic of the miscarriage, then do so. If you make it a manipulated situation, then that will drastically backfire. However, if the conversation is natural, you will be surprised to find that your friend will open up and talk about things that are bothering him.

3. *Ask open-ended questions.* Open-ended questions are questions which cannot easily be answered with a simple "yes" or "no." They push the person to divulge a bit more information. These are questions like, "Tell me about what you have done to process the miscarriage." "What has it been like dealing with the miscarriage?" "How have you and your wife been drawn together through the miscarriage?" These types of questions will draw out the conversation in your friends and allow them to have meaningful conversations with you.

4. *Give him the space and time to process and discuss.* In my personal case, it took me nearly a decade to be ready to discuss what I had been through. For your buddy, it may be the same length of time, or it may be much

sooner. Whatever the length of time, be sure to give him the space and time he needs.

5. *Remind him that you are good with him talking about it.* This seems simple enough, but sometimes he just needs to hear that you are cool with him talking about the miscarriage. He may say, "Okay," and then never say anything. However, knowing that you are cool with it will help him when he is actually ready to share with someone.

What If I Need to Trust Christ?

We stated at the very beginning of this project that this was unapologetically written from a Biblical worldview. In fact, much of this book has drawn on truths and principles found in the Bible. However, you may be reading this and realize that not only do you not really know what a Biblical worldview is, but you also haven't really had any interest in a worldview based on the Bible (or haven't really ever been interested in the Bible). But maybe now you find yourself wondering if there is something missing in your life. Maybe you have come to realize that there is a hopelessness that you feel that you cannot make sense of. Maybe you realize that it is time for you to stop trusting in yourself and, instead, begin trusting in Jesus Christ. If that is you, then this final point is for you.

We addressed this in detail in chapter five so, I will be brief here, but I'll also include Bible verses so you can check me. Jesus Christ is the only solution for any of us. The Bible reminds us clearly that we are lost and hopeless without Jesus Christ and that the eventual consequence of that reality is eternal Hell without Christ (Romans 3:23). That's the bad news. There's good news, though! Jesus Christ came to earth, lived the perfect life we couldn't live, and died in our place (Romans 5:8). In doing that, He paid the price for your sin and my sin. He took your sin and my sin on Himself, and He paid the penalty, which was death (Ephesians 2:4-9). But He didn't just die, He rose on the third day (I Corinthians 15:20-22) (That's why Easter Sunday is such a big deal.). Because He did that, the Bible says those of us who repent and trust Him as our Lord and Savior will have salvation (Romans 10:13).

ADDENDUM

HELP FOR THE PASTOR

Being a pastor is one of the most difficult and most misunderstood jobs in the world. The only way to really understand what goes on in a pastor's life is to have been a pastor and understand what it is like to serve in that capacity. I wanted to take some time at the end of this book to give some help to those who shepherd the flock of God. I know what you are going through, and I have been where you are. If you will allow me, I would love to give you some thoughts that may help you be more effective in your ministry.

Some of you have suffered through the loss of your own child in miscarriage. If that is the case, then I trust that what I am about to share with you will simply be a means of reinforcing what you have already come to realize. For those who have not experienced loss due to a miscarriage, I would like to help you think through some things that will help your ministry. I recognize that, up to this point, we have addressed things from the standpoint of helping men. Some of what we discuss in this chapter will be geared more to the woman than to the man but, by ministering to the woman in this way, you are ministering to the man as well. These are things I learned either by trial and error or by the personal loss we experienced.

Shepherd through Presence.

It is Tuesday evening. You have had a busy two days of ministry and have just sat down for the evening. The phone rings, and you answer it only to hear a quiet voice on the other end, saying, "Pastor, I just wanted to let you know that my wife just had a miscarriage this afternoon. We would appreciate your prayers." What do you do? What do you say in that moment?

If you have never had a miscarriage yourself, you may not know what to do. I know what it was like to call our pastor when we had our first miscarriage. He may not have known exactly what to say or do, but in a church of 350, where we were just young kids, he was so gracious in his response, and then he made sure that he spent time with us, just making sure we were okay. The most important thing, like in every other circumstance like that, is to just be there. You don't necessarily need to say anything profound. You don't need to say anything offensive either. For the couple who has just had the miscarriage, just knowing that someone loves them, is there to care for them, and will listen to them is enough. They don't necessarily need a lot of fuss and attention on them; they just need to know they are not alone, and that God is going to get them through

Some pastors make the mistake of not giving the miscarriage enough attention. You do not have to spend hours with the couple, but you do have to acknowledge the loss and spend the next week or two simply checking on the couple to see how they are doing and if they need anything. That action alone will speak volumes to them.

Shepherd through Honor.

Pastor, let's talk about the elephant in the room: Mother's Day. One of the most sensitive days in the life of a congregation occurs on Mother's Day. I recognize that this day is not the "Biblically consecrated" day that it has become in the United States. However, one of the things you need to keep in mind is that as you begin to recognize certain groups in your church, you must be extremely careful not to be offensive to those in your congregation who have suffered from a miscarriage. If you ever stop to notice, oftentimes when women are absent from your church on Mother's Day, it is because they have experienced loss and are not particularly interested in being reminded of that on Mother's Day. So, what can you do to be aware and not be offensive?

Be intentional in how you honor mothers. You should know ahead of time what you are going to say and how you will honor mothers that are present. On the one hand, you do not want to minimize those women who are present who are mothers by saying we will just honor all women. But you also cannot get into specifics of different kinds of mothers. For instance, you shouldn't honor the youngest mother in the room if that means you may be put into a situation where you are honoring a girl who had a baby out of wedlock as a teenager. So, go into the morning being intentional about what you will say and who you will honor and how you will honor them is important.

If you would like to honor mothers but are nervous about what to do or what to say, you might consider recognizing all mothers, whether they have brought a baby to term or not or whether they have living children or not. This way you recognize the variety of mothers that are in the room without singling out the oldest mother or youngest mother or newest mother. This day can be very sensitive, but that fear of sensitivity does not need to dominate the day.

For the record, the second elephant in the room is Father's Day. And, given that this book is geared towards men, I would encourage you as a pastor to be sure that you are just as intentional when it comes to fathers on Father's Day. The biggest thing is to make sure you are consistent and that your theology informs your actions. These days like Mother's Day and Father's Day can be great encouragements and blessings for your church family.

Shepherd through Remembering.

Every woman knows the due date of her baby. From the time she takes the first test, she has a general idea of when the baby will be due. If she has been to the doctor and has had her pregnancy confirmed, the doctor will give her an idea of a more certain due date. We have already addressed how to shepherd the couple through the miscarriage. However, when it comes to doing something really meaningful and significant, I would encourage you to somehow write down or record the baby's due date. Maybe you have a system for writing cards to people in your church on their anniversaries or birthdays. Adding the due date of the couple's baby and then writing them a card on that date will have incredible meaning to them.

You, as a pastor, should never underestimate the impact writing a card or a note will have on those you shepherd. When you do this for the couple who has had a miscarriage and write them a note on their baby's due date, you will not only show how loving and caring you are, but you will have tremendous opportunity to speak into their lives as you shepherd them through their walk with Christ.

Shepherd through Preaching.

One of the best ways to shepherd your congregation is through the preaching and teaching of God's Word on a faithful basis. You need to shepherd the congregation on how to deal with things such as miscarriage. One recommendation I would have is that you use the Sanctity of Life Sunday each year to highlight various aspects of the sanctity of life. This can include things like miscarriage or other topics that have to do with the sanctity of life.

You know full well as a pastor that our world is continually devaluing life and trying to deemphasize the view of humanity that God has. Therefore, it is up to you to encourage your congregation to have a Biblical worldview when it comes to the sanctity of life. I found this to be one of the most encouraging Sundays for our people. I would encourage you to find different ways to engage your congregation to be challenged Biblically from the pulpit in this area.

Shepherd through Hope.

Whenever tragedy strikes a family's life, it is a process of time before family members can see the good that could come from their situation. A miscarriage is no different. When the couple goes through the miscarriage, it will take time for them to realize what good can come from that. As a pastor, one of the joys you have is to help to give hope through this tragedy. It may not always be easy to see what hope there is, but there has to be hope since our hope is in Christ.

One of the best things you can do, when the time is appropriate, is to encourage the couple to seek ways to bless and encourage other couples who have had or are going through a miscarriage. I remember that, right after our first miscarriage, we encountered several people who were going through a miscarriage. This was such an encouragement to us to be able to have a way of ministering and encouraging others. It helped to take our focus off our own situation and to help focus our attention on ministering to others.

I know that as a pastor, you have so many things you are trying to juggle. You are trying to help so many people in so many situations. The last thing I want to do is to give you one more way to feel like you haven't done your job. However, when it comes to miscarriage, the silent pain is real and your ability to minister to a man and his wife during this time will be invaluable. So, thank you for indulging me to let me share this burden with you as a pastor. Please know that there are many who are praying for you and wanting to encourage you. Our current ministry is designed specifically to help you and your leadership team. If there is some way that IBL could come alongside you or your ministry, please do not hesitate to let us know. You can visit iblministry.org for more information.

ABOUT THE AUTHOR

Dave Deets served in pastoral ministry for over twenty years. He pastored in Farmington, N.M., Littleton, CO, and Caledonia, MI. In 2015, Dave graduated with his Doctor of Ministry degree. He turned his dissertation into a book entitled: Selecting Elders: *A Biblical Guide to Choosing God's Shepherds.* In 2020, Dave joined IBL, The Institute of Biblical Leadership in a full-time capacity. Dave now travels the world helping God's leaders take the next steps they need to take to be the leader God intends them to be through IBL's four ministries of coaching, consulting, counseling, and training. Dave and his wife Kimberly have three living children: Caleb, Andrew, and Rebecca. The family now lives in Taylors, SC.